THE
SECRETS
OF LIFE

A Practical Guide to Day to Day Living

THE SECRETS OF LIFE

A Practical Guide to Day to Day Living

John Alkalay
and
William Trautwein

GATEWAY PRESS, INC.
Baltimore, MD   2000

Please direct all correspondence and book orders to:
Dr. John Alkalay
500 Pondside Dr., Apt. 3-F
White Plains, NY 10067

Library of Congress Control Number 00-135806
ISBN 0-7905691-0-6

Published for the author by
Gateway Press, Inc.
1001 N. Calvert Street
Baltimore, MD 21202

Printed in the United States of America

To my wife, Alanna,
who taught me what it's really
like to love and be loved.
—*John*

To my wife, Doris,
and godsons, Jake and Max.
May God richly bless you
in every way possible.
—*Will*

Contents

About the Authors

Dr. John Alkalay is a licensed psychologist with a practice in White Plains, N.Y. He also works as a school psychologist for the Greenburgh Central School District. He is co-founder of Perfect Life International and does workshops for schools, businesses and individuals which focus on motivation and personal improvement.

Will Trautwein is a writer and businessman in Baltimore, M.D. He is co-founder of Perfect Life International and serves as a consultant to businesses and private individuals in the United States and abroad.

Acknowledgements

John

In order to have written about "The Secrets of Life" we have to learn them first. There have been many people who have contributed both directly and indirectly to the ideas and philosophy of this book.

My debt and gratitude goes out to my family whose lifetime of love, support and sacrifices are greatly appreciated. To my father, who taught me courage, loyalty, and hard work; to my mother, who taught me about self-lessness and kindness; to my grandmother, who showed me spirit and goodwill; to my brother, who has always been there for me as both brother and friend; to my in-laws, who have put up with all of my unique personality quirks.

Thanks also to my friends who have given me a lot to think about during our many conversations about the trials and tribulations of life: Robert Sellers, George P. McGarrity, Joe Augustini, Rich LaFont, Rich and Meredith Steigman, Kirk and Danielle Leach, Martin and Allison Smith, Richard and Liza Henshaw, Bill and Sally Hespie,

Paul Widen, Anthony Palumbo, Bennett Romney, Paul Maggio, Jay and Stephanie Boyarsky, Dr. Stephanie Newman-Levine, Jackie and Mike Sasloff, Chris and Heather Quirk, Laurie Martin, Karen Bucci, Lucille Conklin and Tina Cressent.

Gratitude also goes out to the professional associates who served as mentors, supervisors and valued colleagues: Dr. David Drassner, Dr. Joel Seltzer, Jack Brull, Angelo DaTocco, Nancy Rein-Rafael, Dr. Juliet Lesser and Dr. John Trotta.

Will

I would like to thank first and foremost my family, whose love and support I deeply appreciate: Loida and Paul Trautwein, Steve and Patti Trautwein, Marian Bellan, John and Linda Randolph, Ted and Linda Bellan, Joanna Randolph, and Minnie and Joe Finklea.

Thanks also to my friends who have helped me so much over the years: Paul and Colleen Babinsky, Jim and Ann Rooney, Scott Phillips, Rich Linckorst, Pat Scully, Mike Kmetz, Mike and Cindy Gaval, Greta and George Brown, Paul Brown, Grace and Bill Ford, Mark and Robin Neumann, Neal Braman, Dr. Kramer, Mark and Amanda Milewsi, Dave Illingworth, John and Elizabeth Shaifer, Scott and Stacy Brumbaugh, the Lasky family, Adam Rudo, Jason Abrams, Tony Burgess, Dave Siddons, Ed and Anna Sobrino, Danny and Sharon Pruitt, Jim Kahler, the Green family, Saadat Ullah, Derrick Campbell, Darryl Godwin and Dave Schwartz.

ACKNOWLEDGEMENTS

Thanks also to my doctors, who have kept me in one piece, mentally and physically: Dr. Strauss, Dr. Rosenthal, Dr. Bass, Dr. Baughman, Dr. King, Dr. Rosenberg, and Lisa Gucinski Waterman, Physical Therapist.

Introduction

Why Should You Read This Book?

Most people drift through life like a boat with no destination. They stumble along with some occasional triumphs but with far too many mistakes along the way. Sometimes people learn from their mistakes. Usually, however, they repeat the same errors over and over again. They think that they are making the right choices and most prudent decisions even though things rarely work out as planned. They don't have the kind of relationship that they wanted. They don't have enough money or time to enjoy life. They don't have inner peace. In short, they are unhappy and unfulfilled.

Eventually, people draw some conclusions from their life experiences. After a lifetime of lessons and challenges many people say, "I wish I knew what I know now when I was young." *The Secrets of Life* offers you a different path. It attempts to answers many of life's great questions while saving you the time and energy of learning them through a lifetime of painful experiences. It provides you with practical and succinct answers to everything from "Prosperity" to "Marriage" to "Adversity."

This book does not claim to be a literary masterpiece. It is an invaluable guide to day-to-day living. Whatever your dilemma, the solution lies within the following pages. If you follow the advice in this book you will be healthier, wealthier and happier. Your self-improvement will be incredible. By practicing proven principles set forth herein you will master all facets of daily living. Why learn life's lessons through painful mistakes and trial and error. Read on and become an expert on *The Secrets of Life*.

HAPPINESS

Happiness is about setting up a life that creates positive feelings within you on a consistent basis. The type of positive feelings is unique to the individual. The artist or musician may be happiest when they feel creative. The salesman or stock broker may be happiest when they make a big commission. Others are most happy when spending time with family. Some people find happiness in church or through spirituality. In short, there are many methods to achieve happiness.

What all methods share is that the feeling of true happiness comes from within. An awareness of being loved, loving someone and a sense of accomplishment can all create happiness. Feelings of self-worth, security and fulfillment can also create joy. The key is to find a way to create these types of feelings every day of our lives.

One of the biggest mistakes people make is that they look for things outside themselves to make them happy. They say "all I need is a relationship and I'll be happy." They say "if only I was making more money, I'd have no troubles." Down the road, after these same people get what they thought they wanted they are still not happy. They say "my husband doesn't give me enough attention" or "I still can't afford to live in the house I

1

wanted even with my 30K raise." These people will never achieve happiness because they are not happy within themselves. They are looking for other people or for possessions to make them happy. This rarely works in the long run.

On the other hand, lets look at somebody who is happy within themselves. Compare a rich man sitting in his whirlpool who is worried about a 3% drop in the stock market vs. a poor man who contentedly sits in his old reclining chair, pops open a beer and watches the ball game. Who is more happy at this moment? The poor man is much happier because he is able to feel relaxed while the rich man feels anxious. The moral of the story is that possessions (stock holdings and a whirlpool) do not create happy feelings. A person creates a feeling within themselves.

We are all looking for life experiences which will make us happy. Whether it is a relationship, a job, or a hobby most people gravitate towards experiences that make them feel good. This can work fairly well in many circumstances but some experiences may also bring unhappy feelings. You may love your wife, but not be content in your marriage. You may love your job, but hate the fact that you have to spend 55 hours at the office every week. One of the secrets of happiness is not only to look for happiness through certain experiences, but to learn to change your emotional state so that most experiences can have an element of happiness to them. Perception is the key. Your experiences change a great deal depending how you label them.

For example, lets take a recently married 35 year old man who laments about missing out on the exciting, care free single days. He curses his loss of freedom and wonders if he really made the right decision about getting married. You can see how a negative perception about being married is developing. However, part of this perception is based on a false belief that he would be out carousing every night if he were single. He is probably remembering some of the good times of his twenties and not the more sad times of being drunk, dateless and alone in the early thirties. He is using his perceptions in a negative manner to keep him from being happy in his marriage. It is much more productive to use your perceptions to create a state of happiness rather than a state of regret.

Your emotional state can create your future experiences. While an experience may create a certain state, so too can a state create the type of experience that you want. In our example, the 35 year old man can create a state of happiness by thinking about how good it is to have somebody who loves him and wants to spend time with him. He can also think about the sense of fulfillment he feels being in a committed relationship. He can think about a future family. There are countless perceptions that this man could use to create a state of happiness which will shape his future experiences with his wife. If he sees her as a "ball and chain," he will no doubt be unhappy. However, if he sees his wife as someone he loves and someone (probably the only one) who he will share all his life experiences with, this creates a different view about being married.

One of the secrets to changing your state is to focus on what you have rather than always looking at what you don't have. Focusing on what you don't have is one of the biggest causes of unhappiness. For example, if you make $100,000 and you spend all your time and energy trying to make $200,000 you will not be happy. If you have great friends and enjoy spending time with them, don't take it for granted and only obsess about not being in a relationship. Thank God that you have healthy, happy kids rather than focusing on the fact that there is something missing in your marriage.

Most people find it pretty easy to be happy when their lives are going well. How about when things aren't so great? A failed relationship, the loss of a loved one, getting fired from your job, unmanageable financial stress and many other events may contribute to feelings of anxiety and depression. Is it possible to be happy under such circumstances? Certainly not in the short term. However, if your view of life is not completely short sighted and you have faith in yourself, you will be able to see the sunshine behind the clouds.

The secret when things go bad is to feel hopeful about the future. You can certainly grieve a loss, swear off relationships for a while and plot revenge against your boss. But to dwell on these feelings any longer than necessary is self-defeating. If you feel down about a disaster in your life, it is OK to work through your depression without trying to convince yourself that you are happy when you are really not. However, most people think only about how they feel in the moment when they are depressed. One trick to help you feel encouraged is to imagine your life a year from now. Try to feel optimistic about where you'll be at that time.

If you can't, it's time to think about working on how you feel about life. You may be unduly pessimistic. You may have poor self-esteem which is preventing you from feeling hopeful about the future. If you are in a state where you can not hold onto the future to keep you going and you have no confidence in your ability to cope with unpleasant life events, you may want to consider professional help to help you out of your mess. It may be just the kick start that you need to move you toward using the techniques suggested so far in this chapter.

Lets say you are in a position in life where you have already created conditions that inhibit your happiness and it's not so easy to get out of them. We are not talking about crises here, but rather a condition of chronic mild unhappiness. For example, you may be in a job you hate but have to keep it to help pay the bills for you and your family. You feel locked into your job and those 40 hours per week are not happy times. What is the secret for you? *The trick to being happy most of the time is to focus on the parts of your life that you are happy with.* Spend more time thinking about what you like, what you are good at and what makes you happy. Stop obsessing about the parts of your life that are not what you want them to be. If you are unhappy about certain things, take some actions to change them. Obsessing, thinking and complaining about your situation never helps anything. In our example, a person with a miserable job should focus on why he's working at this job. If it's to support a family he should take pride in himself for the sacrifice. Also, if he is making such a sacrifice, his family is probably worth it and he should focus his thoughts on his family life, not his work life. A lot of people hate their jobs. That's why it's called "work."

Basically there are several areas of life where you can be unhappy or happy. There is your job, your relationship or lack of one, your family and friends, how you spend your free time and your sleep. These areas account for almost all of your time during the week. Assuming that you spend 40–50 hours at work (a tolerable job) and 50 hours sleeping, this leaves you with about 5 hours a day plus the weekend to feel happy.

One of the biggest traps that people fall into that prevent happiness is squandering their free time. They set up a life that is fraught with responsibility. For example, assuming you get home from work at 6 P.M. and finish dinner around 7 P.M., what do you do for the rest of the night? Do you veg out and watch TV (which can be a relaxing and happy time)? Do you have

5

enough energy to go out and do something you enjoy? Probably not. Do you derive some satisfaction out of a particular relationship (spouse, children, friends)? Hopefully you do because the worst fate would be to come home from work dead tired to an unhappy marriage, a take out dinner and a ton of responsibilities (paying the bills, mowing the lawn, etc.) You work like a dog all week and never get a chance to spend and enjoy some of your hard earned salary.

Whether it is a career, your family or your weekly responsibilities and chores, time can be a very limited and precious commodity. If you have arranged your life with very little free time, you had better be getting a lot of happiness from your committed time. However, if you're like most people, you've overburdened yourself with responsibility. This can only create a lot of stress and detract from your overall state of happiness. A major factor of happiness is to arrange a life where you can choose what you want to do with your time. The more time you leave for yourself, the happier you'll be.

The bottom line is that happiness is dependent on a number of factors in your life. You want to create an environment (spouse, family, job, hobbies) that is satisfying and rewarding. However, even if your environment is not ideal, you can still create happiness by working on your internal emotional state. Changing your state is sometimes easier than changing your situation.

Overall, it shouldn't take too much to make a person happy. You can be in a positive state at home watching TV, going out to dinner or spending time with friends. What will prevent consistent happiness, however, is having expectations of life which are too great. If it takes a lot to make you happy (a six figure salary, the best looking spouse and a summer house on the shore), you have less chance of being happy. Even if you attain a lot of what you are looking for, you may be left always wanting more.

Another trap which prevents happiness is never sitting back and enjoying where you've come, only thinking about where you want to be. If you always focus on what you want to get and never think about what you already have, you'll usually be in a state of discontent. The simplest things (like health) are usually taken for granted, but ask somebody who can't walk what they wish for and I'll bet they don't say a million dollars. Appreciating what you have (even if it is not very much) can go a long way towards helping you to feel happy.

Remember, happiness comes from within and if you work on your own internal state, you can create consistent feelings of happiness without having to make wholesale changes in your life.

Changing Rules to Improve Happiness

What is your goal in life? You may say, "I want a million dollars" or "I want to raise my children to be good citizens." You may be desirous of a wonderful relationship or perfect physical health and beauty. All of these goals have one thing in common: they will result in your happiness. Happiness is the real purpose behind your objectives.

Everyone makes their own rules for happiness whether they realize it or not. You are conditioned by your environment. You decide certain circumstances must occur for you to experience joy.

One of the most important secrets of life is that happiness comes from within, not from external events. You can be happy any time you want to by softening your rules. If you decide you'll only be happy if you hit the lottery, you won't be happy that often. A softer rule would be that you'll be happy if you have good health and are looking forward to a steak dinner. Remember there are a billion people in the world who would be thrilled with this. You have both and you're not happy. Why? You have made your rules for happiness too difficult.

Don't be a slave to your subconscious conditioning. Change your rules and you can increase the daily level of joy you experience. Below are a list of common rules and some improved alternatives to increase your overall state of happiness.

1. If I make more money, I'll be happy.
   Better: If I have enough money to meet my basic needs, I'll be thrilled because most people don't have this luxury.

2. I'd be happy if everything in my life would go smoothly.
   Better: There will always be problems in life, so I'll be happy unless there is a tragedy or crisis.

3. I'd be happy if people liked me.
   Better: I'll be happy if I like myself. Nobody else has enough information to judge me anyway.

4. I'd be happy if my husband/wife appreciated me.
   Better: I'll be happy if I act in a virtuous way. Giving will make me feel happy regardless of whether it is appreciated or not.

5. I'd be happy if my spouse spent more time with me.
   Better: I'm grateful that my spouse is working hard to help provide for our family. I feel special when he/she spends our limited free time together.

6. I'd be happy if I could get more things that I want.
   Better: I'll be happy if I can have everything I need.

7. I'll be happy when I retire.
    Better: I'll be happy right now. Life is too short to put off happiness. Postponing happiness until you are old (and possibly not in the best of health) is ridiculous. I'd be happy to sacrifice some $ to be able to enjoy my work.

8. I'll be happy if my children would just listen to me.
    Better: I'll be happy if my children are happy, healthy and well adjusted. I have faith that I have raised my child to use good judgment and I have faith that they will make decisions that will lead to their happiness. If they are happy, I will be happy for them.

9. I'd be happy if I had better luck.
    Better: I won't let circumstances beyond my control determine my happiness. You can't control what happens to you all the time, but you can control how you react to whatever happens. Life isn't fair but I know I'll be able to roll with the punches.

10. In order to stay on top of things and remain happy, I must constantly think and worry about what could go wrong in my life.
    Better: I can still be prepared for the problems in life without worrying about them. Don't turn minor problems into major worries. I'll look at my problems as challenges to overcome and these challenges will make me stronger and help me to grow as a person.

Achieving happiness is the most important endeavor in life. Don't let random circumstances determine your level of joy. By simply following the principles in this chapter, you can achieve a level of happiness beyond your wildest dreams.

CHARACTER

Your most important possession is your character. Everything else in your life is subject to the bludgeoning of chance. Your money, your kids and even your own life can be taken away at any unfortunate moment. People can destroy your reputation. Only you can destroy your character. Your character has a profound effect on your success and happiness in life. Let's discuss this effect below in:

THE TEN PILLARS OF CHARACTER

1. **Perseverance**—Virtually every great success story is highlighted by perseverance. Sylvester Stallone was turned down by a thousand directors before he sold "Rocky." Ernest Hemingway and John Grisham were rejected by dozens of publishers. Abraham Lincoln lost more than half a dozen elections before becoming president. Success is a game of attrition. Life comes easy for virtually no one. Sometimes you'll do everything right and things will end up wrong. It is at these times you must be your most determined. Keep focused on your goals and persevere. Never let life's little mine fields detonate your dreams.

2. **Honesty**—"Honesty is the best policy." Many of the world's most powerful and wealthy people seem to have other ideas. The benefits of honesty are not as obvious as other elements of character. It's for this reason that honesty is so rare in today's world. Becoming more truthful will help you in many ways. If you attain a reputation of honesty, you will have many more business opportunities. People love to deal with someone they can trust. Honesty makes your interactions with other people simpler. If you are a liar, you need too good a memory. You have to remember to keep your stories straight. Finally, if you are truthful you can be proud of who you've become as a person. Honesty is a rare and valued character trait in today's world and should be treasured. Of course, its harder to be honest. Telling someone the truth may not make them happy and may cause you hardship. This is why honesty equals character.

3. **Humility**—Always be humble about your accomplishments. A braggart has very few friends. Let your record speak for itself. Also, humility guards you against overconfidence. If you believe you are invincible, you can make foolish mistakes. Keep yourself in perspective. Although your mother probably thinks so, you're not the greatest thing since sliced bread.

4. **Generosity**—There is no feeling like helping others. Give at least 5% of your income to charity. Spend at least one hour per week helping others. You will get a large return on this investment. You will get the satisfaction of helping those less fortunate. Thinking of someone other than yourself takes your mind off your own worries.

5. **Self Control**—The world is full of wonderful temptations. Everyone has their weakness. Gambling, drinking,

chocolate, etc., aren't dangerous in moderation. Unfortunately, without self-control your indulgences can become addictions. Take steps to temper your vices before they get out of hand. Consider the long-term results of your actions. You may say, "I'm just hurting myself." Are you really? It may help you to control yourself if you take time to remember that your life affects many others. How would your family feel if you ruined yourself through drugs or alcohol? How would you feel if you gambled away Junior's college fund? A moment of sexual indiscretion could destroy your marriage. Keep focused on what's important in life, and you won't let temptation get the best of you.

6. **Kindness**—Many people confuse kindness for weakness. They try to take advantage of a considerate individual. Don't let this deter you from being a good person. Try to avoid those who mistreat you. There are many people who will embrace your caring and respond in kind. Learn to enjoy doing things for other people. The happiness you will feel will be worth the effort.

7. **Hard Work**—Hard work helps to provide order and meaning to life. Find a job you enjoy and perform it to the best of your ability. It doesn't matter whether you're a homemaker, office worker or tradesman. Your job satisfaction is dependent on your effort. "Idle hands are the devil's workshop." The absence of work usually leads to sloth. Many people fall victim to temptation if unoccupied. A hard worker is usually a more productive individual. There is a saying, "If you want a job done, give it to a busy man." Surprisingly, the harder you work the more energy you usually have to undertake life's other activities. Work hard while you are working but don't work all the time.

Character does not mean you are obsessed with work. Strive to lead a balanced life, working hard at your profession but never forgetting your family.

8. **Patience**—There may be no virtue more rewarding than patience. Thinking long-term is one of the great secrets of life. Impatient people are in a constant state of irritation and stress. Don't strive for immediate gratification. Learn to enjoy the process of achieving something. Bring a book with you to doctors' offices and other places where you may have to wait. Learn to relax. If you feel yourself becoming impatient, breathe slowly and deeply. Remember patience is a key factor in happiness.

9. **Bravery**—Life is filled with peril. Death and disease are two legitimate concerns. Shakespeare accurately wrote, "A coward dies a thousand deaths, a brave man just one." Every time you worry about something, physical changes occur in your body as if the event was actually happening. Worry can destroy the enjoyment of life. Your worries can't be eliminated, but they can be reduced. It has been said that fear is an acronym for false evidence that appears real. Your first step in controlling your worries is determining which are legitimate. Most worries never come to pass. They are caused by negative thoughts. Try not to engage in this type of thinking. Force yourself to talk positively and you will gradually begin to think this way. By changing your way of thinking in this manner, your worries will be drastically reduced. Despite positive thinking legitimate worries will remain. The next step is to determine if you are worried about things beyond your control. It is a waste of time and effort to worry about such matters. In these situations it is best to ask for God's help. Pray to God and ask him to lift your burdens. Feel

the weight being removed from your shoulders. Regular prayer has been proven to provide peace of mind. If you are not religious, try to have faith that things will be okay in the long run. Use past examples from your life when you thought things would never work out and yet they did. Occasionally you will find yourself worried about something you can control. Don't procrastinate and postpone action. Remind yourself that virtually any activity is preferable over worrying. Once you take steps to rectify the situation, you'll find your worries will drift away.

10. **Loyalty**—Loyalty is rare in today's world. It is difficult to find someone who will stand by you when the chips are down. If you maintain your reputation for loyalty, you'll stand out in the crowd. You'll be thought of highly and desired as a friend. Loyal people tend to care deeply and enjoy relationships more fully. If you are loyal, there is a greater chance that people will show loyalty in return. If you are not loyal to others, there is a good chance you will not be loyal to yourself. You will not live by any code of ethics and will not find true happiness. Be loyal and you will learn to live life at its fullest.

IMPROVING CHARACTER

Many people mistakenly believe they have no control of their character. This couldn't be more incorrect. You can alter any way of thinking and break any bad personal habits. It is entirely up to you what kind of person you'll become. You are what you do from here on in, not what you've done in the past.

Everyone suffers in life. In some ways suffering builds character but in other ways it destroys it. Many people dealt a bad hand become bitter. If they are mistreated, they decide to mistreat someone else. If you begin to think this way you will begin to die inside. The world is no longer a good place in many ways but there are good people. Don't let the world win. Use adversity to build your character and you'll be rewarded with more happiness than you could ever imagine. Some effective strategies that help build character are listed below:

1. **"That's Not Fair"**—When you get treated unfairly, a common response is to treat others unfairly. First, change your thinking. Life is not fair. When you get scammed or taken advantage of, it's okay to get angry. However, don't expect that you will never get taken advantage of. Think of it like the weather. You don't get mad at "Mother Nature" when it rains. By the same token, don't get mad at "Human Nature" when you get hustled. Rise above the situation. This shows true character.

2. **Set Character Goals**—You no doubt set financial and work-related goals. If you don't, you certainly should. If you want to build your character, you must make it a priority. Set character goals and try to become a better person. Success in this area is worth more than money ever could be.

3. **Develop a Spirit of Appreciation**—Most human beings are naturally unappreciative. They are selfish and suffer from feelings of entitlement. As a result, they don't fully appreciate the blessing of life and the kindness of others. Actively fight this "natural un-appreciation." Each morning, take five minutes and give thanks for all that is good in your life. Live everyday with an "attitude of gratitude." If you are more appreciative, not only will you be a much happier individual, your character will improve tremendously.

POPULARITY

M ost people want to be loved. We are also concerned with what others think of us. Oddly enough, sometimes we wish to be liked by even those that we don't like. Mastering close relationships (lovers, bosses, families) will be covered elsewhere in this book. The focus of this chapter is how people can become well liked without having to kiss ass. The following guidelines of popularity will make you more likable to the public at large. Follow these simple rules and you'll be loved by all.

1. **Listen**—If you want to be liked, become a great listener. The more you listen the more you'll be loved. People love to hear themselves talk. Listen to people closely with an attentive posture and you'll easily make friends. While they're talking, look straight in their eyes. Never interrupt them but when they're done speaking ask them clarifying questions. Being a good listener is not easy. Many people can be quite boring and it is hard to maintain focus. Try to remember that you are making friends by listening to others. You don't learn anything by speaking. Great knowledge is the reward for a lifetime of listening while you'd rather be talking. Following this first and foremost rule would be enough to greatly increase your popularity.

2. **Warm Greeting**—When you meet somebody give them a cheerful greeting and a firm handshake. Smile and look directly into their eyes. Most of all, be sincere when you meet somebody or they will think of you as a phony.

3. **Names**—Become an expert at remembering names and faces. People feel better when you remember them, especially if it is someone you've only met once or twice. Use their name frequently in conversation. It's like music to their ears.

4. **Family**—Ask people about their families. Is everyone in good health? What's new since last time you saw them?

5. **Advice**—Ask people for their opinions. Most people love to give advice. You show people you value their ideas and you also might receive some useful information.

6. **Don't Give Advice**—Unless specifically asked, don't give advice. Don't give the impression that you're a know-it-all. Resist the temptation to recite facts. Don't try to teach people who aren't interested in learning. If they ask you a question, keep your answers succinct.

7. **Don't Talk About Yourself**—Your day-to-day activities are of great concern to you but unfortunately not to many other people. Only your closest friends and family care deeply about your plans. The less you talk about yourself the more you'll be liked by others.

8. **Punctuality**—Punctuality is a lost art, and as a result is often greatly appreciated by other people. It is important to be on time for business and personal appointments. If you are chronically late you are a constant irritant to others. If you are constantly irritating people your popularity will fade.

9. **Never Brag**—Never brag about your accomplishments. Besides displaying insecurity it can be inconsiderate to others. They are concerned with their own problems. Why would they want to hear of your successes? The only people suitable for such information are those that have a stake in your accomplishments such as partners or parents.

10. **Easy Going**—If you want to be likable be an "old shoe." Make a person comfortable when they're around you. Go out of your way to make them relax.

11. **Birthdays**—Try to remember birthdays and other occasions and send cards. These are greatly appreciated. It shows people you care and think about them. A little kindness goes a long way.

12. **Be Optimistic**—Everyone loves an upbeat personality. Try not to complain. By speaking positively you will be more likable to those around you and also you will im- prove your mood. It also pays to be conscious of your facial expression. Smiling makes you more popular and it improves your mental outlook.

13. **Thank You Notes**—The more rare manners are in society, the more valuable they become. Thank you notes were once commonplace but now are extremely scarce. Their scarcity makes them that much more appreciated. Send thank you notes when fitting and your popularity will rise.

14. **Don't Argue**—If you want to be liked don't argue about sensitive subjects. Avoid heated debates around such issues as religion and abortion unless you can be sure your opin- ions won't be taken personally. How many times has your oratory changed someone's position on such subjects? You can always state your views, but don't assume you are right and opposing views are wrong. Don't criticize other's opinions, even if you don't agree.

15. **Admit Mistakes**—Apologize if you make an error. People don't get angry when you make a mistake. They get angry when you don't admit that you are wrong. Don't let your ego get in the way of your popularity.

16. **Passion**—Popular people are passionate about life. If you are excited about life you're more fun to be around. Develop hobbies and be an interesting person.

17. **Don't Gossip**—Don't talk behind people's backs. Many individuals will try to get you to engage in gossip. Such worthless chatter usually gets back to the person criticized. If you are caught talking behind someone's back they never will like you in the same way again. The camaraderie you share with the gossip is not worth this risk or the stain on your character.

18. **Sense of Humor**—If you want to be well liked, try to develop a sense of humor. Don't take yourself so seriously. You don't have to be a court jester, but an occasional light-hearted remark makes you pleasant to be around. Self-deprecating humor is particularly effective in making you popular. It makes others feel more comfortable around you because you are more comfortable with yourself. Making fun of yourself also never offends anyone like jokes that are racially or sexually oriented.

19. **Loyalty**—Most people realize that friendship counts most in times of strife. Many so-called friends disappear when the chips are down. If you are there for people when they need you most, they will appreciate it more than you'll ever know. If you develop a reputation as a loyal friend you'll be rewarded with true devotion.

20. **Appearance**—It may seem odd to say but appearance has a lot to do with popularity. People tend to like attractive people. Of course not everyone can be handsome or

beautiful. Try to dress nicely and have good hygiene. Don't let your popularity be damaged by people's prejudices.

21. **Compliments**—Never miss an opportunity to bestow a deserved compliment. People crave positive reinforcement. When you compliment them you are showing them you appreciate their efforts.

22. **Control Anger**—Anger is sometimes unavoidable. However, frequent angry outbursts can greatly hinder your popularity. No one can force you to become angry. You have the power to control that emotion. If you feel yourself getting angry politely leave the room. Return and continue the discussion when you calm down. If you try to consider the other person's point of view it can help the situation. If you determine they're trying to irritate you, you should not give them the satisfaction of seeing you upset.

23. **Flamboyant Expressions**—Many of the most popular individuals have an engaging method of conversation. Develop a stable of flamboyant expressions. You will be seen as a more interesting person. The more interesting you are, the more popular you become.

24. **Manners**—As was stated earlier, in this day and age, if you have manners you will stand out above the crowd. Become an expert on etiquette. Be polite and you will be popular.

25. **Golden Rule**—"Do unto others as you would have them do unto you." Extremely few people follow the golden rule. It insists that you are always considerate of other people. In today's world, you would be a diamond in the rough.

In many ways your most important legacy when you leave this world is the impression you leave behind. No one but your heirs will care how much money you have made. If you are not liked, who will grieve for you at your funeral? If no one cares that you have died, what have you really accomplished? There is a saying that goes "to achieve immortality, live a life that's worth remembering." The best way to be remembered is to have made an emotional impact on people. If you work on implementing the tips from the above list, you will be loved while you're alive and fondly remembered even after you're gone. Learn these 25 easy methods and you'll master the secret of life known as **popularity**.

L<u>UCK</u>

That's the way the cookie crumbles. It's better to be lucky than good. Life isn't fair. These popular sayings illustrate the role of luck in our lives. What is luck? Luck can be defined as circumstances that happen to us beyond our control (both good or bad). Whether this luck is caused by some force of fate or by pure randomness is immaterial. Most people don't recognize the role of luck in their lives because it makes them feel powerless. They are missing out on one of the great secrets of life. While you can't master fate, you can shape good and bad luck.

If you are reading this book, chances are that you have incredible luck in your life. You may not think of yourself as very fortunate. You might have financial or relationship problems or perhaps physical ailments. You may compare yourself to others who seem more happy and successful. Don't look at the glass half empty. A quarter of the world's population is starving. The unfortunate people who live in those areas are sentenced to a life of poverty without committing a crime. No matter how hard they work there is very little hope. To be born in North America or Western Europe is an incredible windfall. Ninety percent of the world's population is born elsewhere. Even if you are in the lucky ten percent, you could suffer from physical, emotional or mental handicaps. You could be the victim of physical or sexual abuse. If you don't suffer from any of these calamities you are incredibly lucky.

Even though you are already fortunate, it may be hard for you to "feel lucky." There are several steps you can take to promote even better luck.

THE THREE KEYS TO GOOD LUCK

1. Build a large network of friends and contacts. Extroverts usually have better luck than introverts. Learn to enjoy dealing with other people and building relationships. It is impossible to know which people will offer you opportunities in the future. It is clear the more friends you have the better your chances. Friends can also help when you are a victim of bad luck and provide a buffer of safety from catastrophe.

2. Take risks that don't have a big down side. Gamblers, not lucky people, gamble their money on one roll of the dice. Even if you win, which you probably won't, you'll take the same risks again down the road. Don't make grandstand plays. They work in the movies but generally not in real life. However, you should take chances that don't have a big down side risk. For example, if you are in a dead end job and somebody comes to you and offers you a business partnership in an exciting field with little capital investment required, why not seize the day? If the business fails you can usually return to your former position, and if not, you can find a similar job in your field. Most people do not recognize good luck when it comes their

way until it's too late. Keep an eye out for good fortune and seize it when it presents itself.

3. Do what works for you. The world works in mysterious ways. Some people are simply better and luckier at some endeavors than others. Many individuals, especially men, can't admit they lack talent in a certain area. The male ego hampers them. Concentrate on your strengths not your weaknesses. If you do you will have a luckier result.

Dealing with Bad Luck

Sometimes you will do everything right and it will still end up wrong. The feeling of being unlucky is one of the world's most troubling emotions. Matters are made worse because bad luck seems to appear in streaks. During one of these unlucky streaks you have the feeling that a grand piano is on your back. Nothing seems to work out properly. Here is where most people seem to make a critical error. They make rash moves and decisions in an attempt to change their luck. They know that if they take a big chance and it works out they will no longer feel unlucky.

The worst time to take chances is when you're in a cold streak. Luck ebbs and flows for everyone. You must be patient and confident in the fact that your fortunes will improve. People exacerbate their bad luck in other ways. If you are a victim of bad luck it is important that you don't let it change your behavior. Consider this example of two farmers: Shortly before the harvest, a storm ruins both the farmers' fields. Farmer Brown says to himself, "That is bad luck but it's the business. Every twenty years or so the harvest will be ruined by a fluke frost. I have saved money to deal with such an unfortunate event and look forward to better times next year."

Farmer Tom is enraged at his bad luck. "How could this happen the night before the harvest?" All his hard work has been ruined. What has he ever done to God to deserve such bad luck? His anger causes him to fall off the wagon and begin drinking alcohol again. His wife, fed up with his drinking, leaves him and takes his kids. The loneliness forces him to seek the comfort of prostitutes. Unprotected sex with these prostitutes leads to his infection with HIV.

Why did the unfortunate frost ruin the life of one farmer and not the other? *The answer is that when bad luck strikes you, you must think long term. If you think short term, unlucky streaks can get the best of you.* When something bad happens to you, ask yourself if it will affect you three or five years down the road. Has any permanent damage been suffered. Most bad luck just causes temporary inconvenience. Examine your bad luck for lessons learned. What seems like bad luck in the short term can be good luck in the long term. Bad luck can offer you invaluable life experience. You often can be a better, smarter, wiser person because of misfortune.

Count your blessings. You are a lucky person. If something goes wrong don't necessarily blame yourself. There are many circumstances over which you have no control. If you are a victim of bad luck don't panic and exacerbate the situation. Think long term and remember things are not as bad as they seem. Today's travails will probably have no effect on you in the future. Remember fortune ebbs and flows, be optimistic and by all means—**good luck.**

DATING

How to Meet Somebody?

Many people have the mistaken impression that there is nobody out there. They've tried all the obvious methods (bars, personal ads, set ups from friends) with limited success. After a while, singles can start to feel bitter and hopeless. They can recite story after story about the latest crazy person they dated. Even through the trying times, singles never give up. They are always willing to go out on another date in hopes that it will be the one that works out.

The problem with meeting people to date is not due to lack of effort, but rather to misplaced effort. Most singles in their 20's and 30's continue to try the weekend bar scene to meet someone. Every once in a while they get a date, but mostly they just end up buzzed. Bars happen to be one of the worst places to meet someone. Guys may have had a few drinks and are not at their charming best. Women think guys are just out for sex and are very guarded and mistrustful during conversations.

This mistrust and suspiciousness between singles is very hard to overcome. This is why personal ads have such a low rate of success. When singles contact a personal ad, they wonder why a person would have to resort to placing an ad. Many times they are charged a few dollars to contact an ad and their call is not even returned. Even if a meeting is eventually arranged, it ends up being an uncomfortable, forced situation that is hard to overcome even if the two people are fairly well matched.

The Internet has added a new dimension to personal ads. It is somewhat less threatening because much of the contact can be done through chats and E-mail. However, even if your e-mailing is going well, all you know is that your prospective "personal" can write well. You have no idea what they look like or if they come across in person as well as on the computer. He or she may be a poet who looks like a troll.

Blind dates have some of the same risks. Most times you don't even know if you'll be attracted to your date. If you go this route, be sure to trust the person who is setting you up and go in with realistic expectations.

Many singles try to go out as much a possible thinking the more they date, the better the odds of meeting someone special. This can be a very frustrating, expensive and time consuming process. In the end, singles end up disappointed and disillusioned by who they meet.

The bottom line is to stop wasting time, effort and money on trying to meet someone. It is much easier to find someone if you're not looking. This is not to say you don't put yourself in situations where meeting someone is possible but you don't have to actively seek it out. Singles should not feel like they have to "be on" every time they are around other singles. Meeting someone and getting dates should not feel like work.

One of the secrets of meeting someone is to put yourself in social situations where you are out doing something you like.

The key is to do something that you enjoy so you don't even have to think about meeting somebody even if there is a lot of people around. For instance, if you like fitness, don't just be a gym rat waiting for someone to talk to. Try to take a class of some sort whether it be aerobics or kick-boxing. Join a running club and go to several races. Take group tennis lessons. Even if you never talk to anyone, you will have had some fun. Chances are you can meet someone where there might be a physical attraction and a common interest.

If you like more intellectual pursuits, join a book club, go to a poetry reading or take an adult education course in a subject of interest. The idea is to be active, do as many fun activities as your schedule allows and put yourself in situations where you'll have a chance to interact with people of the opposite sex who share common interests.

You should not be taking a dance class if you hate to dance just for the sake of trying to meet someone. Do things that you like to do, try something new and meeting people will naturally follow. Furthermore, if you are doing an activity, conversation is easy because you share a common interest and can talk about this topic with no pressure. In addition, you can get a better feel of who you might like because you are seeing the same people on a consistent basis.

The biggest problem is that most singles are too lazy or too scared to try something new. They stick with bars and set ups rather than going to a cooking class or joining a ski club. It is crucial to stop wasting your time to meet someone in the wrong places. Start looking into social activities you may enjoy. It will be fun at the very least and you have a better chance of meeting someone.

How a Man Can Make Himself As Attractive As Possible

Attraction is a difficult area because it is very subjective. Your physical appearance and/or personality can attract one woman and repel another. While many types of attraction are fairly subjective, there are some secrets as to what most women find attractive in men (even if they would never admit it).

First of all, *most women are attracted to men with confidence.* Whether you are quiet and self-assured or outgoing, charming and poised, feeling good about yourself is one of the most attractive qualities in a man. If you come across as insecure and unsure of yourself you will turn off most women. If you think you are attractive and worthwhile, other people will think so too, but if you are unsure of yourself most people will be unsure of you.

Another quality that most women find attractive is financial security. Many women would never admit that money is important to them. However, how often do you see an unemployed man living with parents dating an attractive and personable woman. That is not to say that all women want a rich guy, but almost all women want a comfortable and secure life. They just want to feel secure that if the relationship grows into something beyond casual, the man has a stable, steady salary. Thus, for some women, a teacher's salary is OK, but others want you to make six figures or you have no chance. For almost all women, the guy who has been floating from job to job with no direction and/or is currently working in a dead end job has no chance. As sad as it may be, money (and the security that comes with it) attracts.

Another way to be attractive to women is not to go overboard acting nice. Being too complimentary, overly considerate and always agreeable is not what they are looking for. In fact, this may come across as too nice and may be looked upon with suspicion by women. They may think you are not being real.

Even worse, however, is the fact that many women often mistake kindness for weakness. If you are not a nice guy you should have no conflicts in this area. However, if you are nice, considerate and sensitive by nature you may be turning off some women without even knowing it. Granted, these are terrific qualities to have once you are in a relationship but there is no need wear these emotions on your sleeve on the first date. For example, asking a woman what she would like to do and/or where she would like to go on a first date may seem like a considerate gesture. However, what may come across is that you are not able to plan a good date yourself and you need her help to find things to do.

This is not to say men should act in a selfish and rude manner when planning dates. After planning the date, the considerate man can always ask, "Is this OK with you?" However, knowing what you want, where you want to go and when you want to do it are looked on favorably by women. They see this as a sign of strength, confidence and assertiveness.

Fortunately for men, one area which you do not have to worry too much about is your looks. You can dress in nice clothes and get a nice haircut, but ultimately you look like you no matter what you do. Furthermore, many women do not rely on looks as much as men do in finding a partner.

Even though looks are not the top priority to most women, your physical attractiveness will have some implications as to the type of women that you will be able to date. However, *the type of woman that will be attracted to your kind of look is out of your control so there is no need to worry about it.* Knowing that you can't do much about how you look or who is going to be physically attracted to you should come as a huge relief. Furthermore, men should be grateful when they are turned down by a woman doesn't feel attracted to them. You won't get your hopes up only to have them dashed later. You find out where you stand right away.

Many men wish they could be taller, have a better build or a more handsome face. Granted, your pool of potential dates is increased if you are extremely handsome, but the beauty of dating is that all you really need is for one person who you really like to like you back. You never know who will be attracted to you. Believe it or not, there are some women attracted to certain qualities in men that would not commonly be thought of as attractive (e.g. some women go for bald guys).

Once you determine that someone is not interested in you, stop wasting time with her. *One of the worst things that men try to do is to try and make somebody become attracted to them.* You should not have to sell yourself. Attraction should happen naturally. Often, men spend money, time and effort trying to persuade a woman what a great guy they are. After three dates and a few hundred dollars, they hear the famous last words, "Let's just be friends." Instead, why not pay attention to the signals that she might not be interested and move on.

How a Woman Can Make Herself As Attractive As Possible

The first secret that women already know is that men place a high priority on physical attractiveness. However, physical attractiveness is based on more than just looks. It is also based on how you carry yourself (confidence) and your sexuality.

Many women fall into the trap of spending a great deal of time on shopping for clothes and putting on expensive make-up thinking this drastically changes their appearance. They read up on the latest fashions. They take two hours to get ready for a date. They change their mind five times before deciding which outfit to wear. Don't spend hours on something which makes very little difference. *When your wear the most fashionable outfit, the only ones who will really notice it are other women.* For the most part, men don't know a thing about fashion. They can tell if an outfit looks horrible, but most men would never be able to distinguish between a $50 outfit and a $250 outfit. Women should dress nicely, but don't overdo it and stop wasting so much time with it.

If you want to waste time with something that will make you attractive to men, try familiarizing yourself with some of the things men find interesting. *For instance, knowing about sports is an extremely attractive quality to many men.* You don't have to memorize the batting averages of every major league hitter and should be very wary of any man who knows this as well. It would be very endearing, however, if you rooted for a particular team or if you were actively involved in sports. Any woman that can have a nice conversation about sports on a date scores a lot of points with most men.

Listening (and asking questions) is an underrated quality that is very attractive to most men. Women (or men) who talk about themselves 99% of the time are very unappealing. Many women complain that men do not like to talk about their feelings. This is untrue. It's just that many women don't know how to get men to talk about their inner thoughts. The reason for this is that they focus their questions on how a man feels about something because that is what they would want to be asked about themselves.

A better way to get a man to open up is to ask him about things that make him feel important and successful. *Men are driven by their ego.* When talking about an accomplishment, something they do well or something they are very knowledgeable about men feel both important and special. One of the best ways to be attractive to men is to make them feel important. This does not mean making overly flattering statements or telling them how great they are. This quality is very unattractive and is something that no self-respecting woman would want to do anyway. However, if you can ask questions in a subtle way and it is part of your nature to be curious about another person's life, you come across as a caring, interested person. As a bonus you will be massaging a man's ego without even trying and he will be more likely to open up emotionally.

Another very attractive quality to men is women who have interests outside of relationships. Many men are worried that a woman will become too attached to them in a relationship. She will want to spend every free moment with her boyfriend. Men are on the look out for women who come across as too needy. To make yourself as attractive as possible, it is important to have an independent side. This can be a career or a particular area of interest that you pursue with passion. Men love it when a woman has independent interests that don't necessarily involve them. It could be volunteering once a week at a retirement community or belonging to an investment club.

Dating Strategy

There are NO RULES that need to be followed when dating someone. You don't need to worry about when you should call back after the first date or how many dates to wait before your first kiss. You only have to do what feels right to you. Don't base your actions on how you think it will come across to your date because you will never know.

How many times have you wondered what your date thought about something you did. Did she like the restaurant that you picked? How did he feel when I didn't invite him in after the date? It's impossible to know what somebody is thinking, but singles try to figure this out all the time. Many singles obsess over the meanings of their actions and the behaviors of their dates.

The problem with this approach is that you can never figure out why people do what they do. Many times people do something and have no idea why they did it. For example, on a third date you find that you start to fool around at the end of the night and get very good impressions of where things are heading. On the fourth date you feel that a wall is getting put up and things seem to regress. You wonder why, consult your friends and come up with possible conclusions about why your date is backing off. One friend thinks the person might have intimacy issues. Another friend thinks the person is crazy. A third just thinks you should slow things down. You end up agreeing with one of these interpretations and act accordingly. Let's say that you take the advice to slow things down and don't set up a date for a couple of weeks. The result could be that your date feels slighted and has less interest in seeing you (not more as you had thought).

Unfortunately, there is no way to figure out what the right thing to do is and how your actions will affect someone else's feelings. People are much too complicated for this and your information about them is far too limited to try and figure them out in the first place. Thus, if you plan how to go about dating based on what you think the other person will think, you will usually be wrong. The solution is not to worry about strategy and not to obsess about what your date is feeling and thinking. Just do what feels right and fun for you and pay more attention to how you are feeling. You will act more naturally and be more genuine this way.

Once you realize that there is very little you can control when you are trying to start a relationship, you'll feel much less pressure. Additionally, you won't feel as bad if it doesn't work out. *One of the hardest things is to let go of the feeling that you can control, manipulate or change how somebody feels about you.* If you are willing to acknowledge that there are so many things in dating that you can do very little about, you will end up much happier. Just go out, have a good time and let the chips fall where they may.

Game Playing

Everyone hates game playing. Yet so many people do it. Why? Either they are emotionally troubled, confused, manipulative or just plain mean. Furthermore, when people feel that they are "being played," they usually respond by playing back. This sets up a vicious cycle and both people end up hurt and/or angry.

What you should do when you feel that your date is playing games with you is to choose not to play. If you think someone is playing games with you, don't set yourself up or use some lame strategy to get back at them. Realize that all these dating games are ways for people to feel like they are in control. Be on the watch for these people and do not get involved with them. Below are some typical "game players."

1. **Emotionally Disturbed/Crazy**—Usually, these people are very charming and sometimes very good looking. This is what gets you hooked in. Things get intense quickly. Shortly after, when intimacy and/or sex starts to become a factor the craziness starts to surface and things go awry. If you sense someone having some trouble with basic intimacy, this is a sign of trouble.

2. **Scumbags**—Male scumbags are just after sex. They will do anything or say anything to get you into bed. Usually, they show you a good time and are very aggressive. If you end up sleeping with them, they'll become uninterested shortly after. Female scumbags are those women that never plan to have sex with you. They'll be very friendly and give off fake signals that they are interested and talk about sex quite a bit. After you have spent a lot of money taking them to fancy dinners and try to kiss them, they'll say they aren't interested in you in that way. Thus, women should be careful about sleeping with someone until you trust his intentions. Men should kiss a woman good bye if they haven't gone any further than a goodnight kiss after a couple dates.

3. **Losers**—They may be very nice people but they have limited social skills, no sense of humor, nothing interesting to talk about and quite possibly poor hygiene habits. You realize this in two minutes. Finish your cup of coffee or dinner and get out of there.

4. **Bad Boys**—These guys have a hard edge to them. Being with them feels exciting and intense. This type does not like to settle down, but they have a way of drawing women into thinking that they can change him. Bad boys are great for short term flings, but be careful about getting sucked into something that will seem serious to you but not for him.

5. **Sluts**—These women can be exhilarating for men because they ooze sexuality in a sleazy but desirable way. Men's minds are on sex from the start and there is usually a quick transition from dates to having sex—maybe even on the first date. If your hard up, this may be great for a short term fling. However, if you are getting easy access to sex so is everyone else. Wear a condom at all costs. Beware of the HIV factor. Having to worry about AIDS is not worth having sex no matter how good it is.

6. **The Professional Dater**—This type is usually a very charming man who seems to know all the "in" places to go out and knows all the right things to say. The first date always goes extremely well because these guys are silky smooth. The risk is that women become emotionally in-volved with this type of guy before they realize that they are just being used and end up getting hurt. If you want to be treated well and shown a good time this is OK in the short term. Remember though that they'll be out the door at the first sign of intimacy.

Dealing with Rejection in Dating

Fear of rejection is one of the biggest factors that interferes with successful relationships. It prevents men from asking out women in the first place. It prevents women from letting men know they are interested.

Let's use the analogy of a fruit stand to explain some of the principles of rejection. There are many fruits to be picked at a fruit stand. If you think of yourself as an apple and you're not chosen by somebody because they like oranges better, why should you take it personally. Many people would think of themselves as a rotten apple instead of seeing it as that particular shopper prefers oranges, but there will be others who will like apples. Everyone has different tastes. Even if you're not chosen often because you are a somewhat uniquely shaped, quirky and exotic fruit such as a papaya, you'll eventually find someone who loves papayas. Just don't take yourself off the shelf so there's no chance.

In other words, there's no need to take getting turned down personally. There are a myriad of reasons why someone might not be interested in you. Maybe they're not physically attracted to you. Maybe they're not interested in dating. Too bad, but no big deal. Whatever the case, the reason people end up feeling bad is because they see the whole package as betting rejected. It's not just their looks but their personality and their overall character as well.

Getting turned down based on a brief conversation has nothing to do with you—so don't feel bad about it. If it's due to physical attraction, it's out of your control. If it's due to the impression that you made, just remember that the person only has a small glimpse of your personality from which to draw a conclusion, so they are only turning down a first impression.

Even if you stop seeing one another after several dates, it still says nothing about your self worth. People that feel only disappointment when a situation doesn't work out will feel bad but will recover quickly. People that feel both disappointed and hurt may feel lousy for quite a while. They feel hurt because they interpret rejection as their date telling them that they are "no good." They lament about why they were dumped. Was it because of looks? Did they do or say something wrong? Were the dates not interesting enough? People end up torturing themselves in hindsight and wonder what they could have done differently to keep things going with someone they really liked.

The simple truth is that when things don't work out, it's because of chemistry or emotional feelings not based on any logic. Maybe a woman reminds a man of his mother (emotion). Maybe a women decides not to date a man because she doesn't appreciate his sarcastic sense of humor (chemistry). You can take rejection personally, get depressed and let it affect how you feel about yourself or you can chalk up things not working out to more circumstantial factors (which you could have never have done anything about in the first place).

Overall, dating is a lot less complicated than singles make it out to be. Hopefully, the secrets in this chapter can help you move on to the next stage—a relationship.

RELATIONSHIPS

Beginnings

The transition from dating to a relationship is not always smooth sailing. It is marked by uncertainty, anticipation, excitement and sometimes disappointment. Couples go through uncharted waters together with no idea where things will lead. Powerful feelings start to develop between a couple when they are becoming closer. The struggle to become more intimate is fraught with many roadblocks.

The first area of difficulty is the feeling of uncertainty. People often don't know what they want in a relationship. They base the state of the budding relationship solely on how they feel at any given moment. When they feel intimate, excited and passionate they think the relationship is the best thing in the world. However, when something happens that makes them feel threatened, hurt, angry or disinterested they tend to pull back. There is rarely a smooth progression to intimacy but the road is even rockier if you are confused about what you want and/or how you feel about someone.

In most cases, couples rarely like each other equally at the beginning of a relationship. Usually, one person is more excited about the relationship than the other. *The one who is more excited usually pushes to get closer and the one who is less excited pulls back.* The pushing and pulling may rotate from one partner to the next in some relationships if both partners are unsure of their feelings.

Another problem at the beginning of a relationship is caused by differing feelings about how slow or fast to move the relationship. For example, one partner may want to have an "exclusive" relationship and the other wants to continue to see other people. The partners may have differing views about sex. One partner may want to spend every weekend together.

Negotiating these differences often determines the success of the relationship. Skills in communicating how you feel are important at these times. Even more important is taking your partner's feelings into account. In most cases, the more considerate you are, the more consideration you will get back. If this does not happen to be the case, you may want to re-consider your relationship and/or bring the topic up for discussion.

One of the biggest secrets of beginning relationships is to understand that the more you have to push to get closer, the more you will drive your partner away. Most people "push" because they get anxious. Most people pull back because they feel scared, threatened or they begin to lose interest. If they have lost interest there is nothing you can do. However, if you want to get closer to someone who seems scared, give them a little space and things tend to fall into place. Have a little faith, confidence in yourself and optimism about the relationship.

Another common pitfall at the beginning of a relationship is that people always try and interpret the meaning of what their companion says or does. They waste countless hours consulting with friends about the fact that it's Wednesday and their partner hasn't called them back about plans for the weekend. Does it mean they are losing interest? Not necessarily. Maybe they are trying to plan something exciting and the details aren't worked out yet. Maybe they have a work project that's keeping them in the office until 11 P.M. every day. *The point is that you have no clue why somebody does something unless they tell you. Stop trying to figure it out. You do not have enough history in your new relationship to know their motives and you have no context in which to try and frame what they did.* Furthermore, it's usually something that's not worth obsessing over. Either you'll get the call before the weekend or you won't. In either case, you will have learned more about your partner's character by the way they handle things.

Another big mistake that people often make at the beginning of a relationship is to mistake charm for character. Your dates are exciting and the person always seem to know the right things to say. Because they are so charming, you tend to ignore some warning signs which may give you important information about their character. For example, the charmer may speak very sincerely about how he or she worked for the homeless on Thanksgiving one year and you think about how caring and selfless that person must be. However, is the person really this wonderful or is he or she just trying to impress you? You just don't know until after you see first hand how they treat you. A great verbal resume does not always equal a great person. It takes some time to find out about loyalty, integrity and responsibility. *Your character is based on what you do, not by what you say.*

Another trap to watch out for is not to mistake passion and lust for love. One of the most misleading sayings of all time is, "It was love at first sight." Nothing could be further from the truth. However, it may very well have been "lust at first sight."

43

When people are beginning a relationship, there is often a lot of passion which culminates in sex and more sex. Many people mistake sex as symbolic of some deeper feeling—such as love, intimacy, etc. However, often it is just sex. Many men (and some women) are just out for sex. Sometimes this is hard to recognize and women sometimes mistake their sexual encounters as a sign that the relationship is growing closer. Men may be very passionate in the short term but once the lust wears off, the relationship may not get any closer. Fortunately, if you followed the tips in the dating chapter you will not find yourself in this unfortunate predicament after a month or two of dating someone.

Even when two people are committed to giving a relationship a try, sex may cloud their judgment. When a couple is having passionate sex, there is usually an accompanying emotional high. This "high" tends to make people ignore a lot of qualities in their partner which may have more importance in the long term success of the relationship. Once the newness of the relationship starts to wear off a little, you start to see more clearly. Hopefully, the more you see the more you like but this is not always the case.

Many people tend to overlook character flaws, especially at the beginning of a relationship. Unfortunately, these overlooked shortcomings are often cited as reasons for a divorce years later.

Example # 1: Jack & Jill

Jill is an attractive, young woman who has plenty of suitors. The young men interested in her are often kind and attentive but that seems to repel Jill. Jill equates kindness with weakness. She also finds that all the attention and praise she receives from these men turns her off. She does not see these guys as much of a challenge.

When Jill meets Jack, his disinterest excites her. She notices that he has an extremely bad temper, but she thinks that this is a sign of strength and assertiveness. Besides, he certainly must love her if he gets that angry and jealous when he is with her.

Jack has a good job, is well built and handsome. He is also undependable and drinks too much but Jill tends to overlook these factors as unimportant. Jack doesn't treat Jill especially well but she thinks she can change this pattern over time.

Ultimately, these two decide to get married. Five years later Jill is fed up with the marriage and in a deep depression. How could this happen to her? She has an angry husband who doesn't treat her well. He drinks too much and is undependable. He is disinterested and never pays any attention to her.

Her husband is the same jerk she fell in love with five years ago. Now she hates him and feels victimized. She "wasted" all those years. Jill was always aware of Jack's character flaws but chose to overlook them during their courtship. Now those same shortcomings are cited at the divorce proceedings.

Example # 2 Fred & Ginger

Fred is dating a gorgeous girl named Ginger. She has the body of a model and the face of an angel. Fred knows his friends are impressed and envious that he is dating such a beautiful girl.

Ginger likes to wear sexy outfits and gets a lot of attention from men. The fact that so many men want to be with Ginger excites Fred. It is a big ego boost for him.

Ginger is also very spoiled and selfish because men have always catered to her every whim. Fred has dated several women that have treated him very well, but none of these ladies were as sexy as Ginger. They were loyal, kind and supportive but perhaps a few pounds overweight.

Ginger, however, has the perfect body. Fred doesn't mind that Ginger is being selfish and unappreciative because he gets to make love to her and she seems to like his companionship. Fred and Ginger get married.

Five years later, Fred can't stand Ginger. She always acts selfishly and never appreciates anything he does for her. No matter how hard Fred works at making Ginger happy, he can't seem to please her. Ginger flirts with other men and loves to wear sexy clothing. Fred has grown tired of men (especially his friends) hitting on his wife.

Ginger is still a knockout physically but Fred is no longer excited by her. He has no interest in sex with his "beautiful" wife. Ultimately, he files for divorce.

Fred knew from the very beginning that Ginger was spoiled, selfish and unappreciative. He chose to ignore these character traits because she was so beautiful and she made him feel so good about himself.

Why do people overlook character so often in relationships? The answer is that they choose their partner for sexual reasons much of the time. While sexual passion subsides over time, the emotional intimacy based on character can last a lifetime. This is what will ultimately determine the success of the relationship.

We offer these words of caution, fully realizing that natural instincts (lust, attraction, greed, passion, etc.) often draw you towards making serious mistakes in relationships. Strong emotions can cause havoc on reasoning and logic. Ask yourself if you would still be with your partner when the sex life and passion cools off (sooner or later it will!!). Does your partner's character traits make you love him or her even more or are you overlooking some fatal flaws? Answering this question accurately may be the key to determining the long term success of your relationship.

Overall, the beginning stage of the relationship can be the most thrilling part. If you know how to deal with your anxiety and can enjoy the feelings you are having without getting lost in them you have a great chance of moving to the middle stage.

Middle

The middle stage is marked by a sense of comfort in the relationship. You have passed all the beginning hurdles and are now in an exclusive relationship which has lasted several months. You have made the decision to be in a relationship and are now faced with the dilemma of how serious you want to get.

Some people go into a relationship hoping it will lead to marriage. Others are in it for the fun of getting close but have no intention of getting married. This is often a matter of age, timing, maturity and emotional stability.

The idea of getting serious is a stage of life issue. It can be different for men and women. For men, the early to mid-twenties are a time of learning about what you like and what you want in a relationship. Career is often a priority. Often, a girlfriend is just thought of as a girlfriend, not as a future wife. Looks tend to be a crucial factor in deciding who men want to be with at this stage.

For women, the goals of the early to mid twenties, are often very similar to those of men. Women are often thinking about advancing their education and/or career. While it would be nice to have a boyfriend during these times, it is not a crucial consideration nor are boyfriends always looked at as husband material. Things tend to change in the mid to late twenties. Usually, women tend to get more serious about relationships before men. Men seem not to get serious until the late 20's or early 30's.

During the middle stage, people often wonder if they are in love or not. It is not always an easy question to answer because there is no logic to it. You may be going out with what you thought was the man of your dreams, but you sense that something is missing. You can't put your finger on it because he is a great guy, treats you well and is heads over heels in love with you. Even though you should be in love, you're not.

Love is a very individual and unique feeling. Everyone experiences it in his or her own way. It simply comes down to how you feel. If you have to analyze it too much, it's not love. If you don't know how you feel, give it some time. Some people experience love after a few weeks and for others it make take months before they discover that they are in love.

It is a very common issue for people in the middle stage of a relationship to wonder about love. You may wonder if you are in love. You may wonder if your partner is in love with you. You may wonder if, when and how you will tell your significant other that you are "in love" with them.

Love is not as easy a feeling to identify as happiness. You usually know when you are happy and exactly what is making you happy. Your relationship may be making you happy and you can describe exactly why to others. It's not as easy with love. You may know you are in love but it is not easy to explain why.

In the end, love is very simple. Either you feel it or you don't. Unfortunately, falling in love is the easy part. Staying in love takes some work.

Contemplating Marriage

This stage occurs in serious, committed relationships only (hopefully). The idea of marriage can bring thoughts of love, intimacy, contentment, fulfillment and family. We hope to find a soul mate, someone who brings out the best in us, who can support us through hard times and share the joy of good times.

Yet many times relationships do not measure up to this ideal standard. The loving feelings you have toward your partner may be wonderful but they often fall short of your fairy tale version of love and marriage. This may create some doubts and anxiety about getting married. Some of the most common fears and barriers that get in the way of potential marriages are:

1. Maybe I could do better.
2. What if it doesn't work out.
3. A divorce would ruin my life.
4. I'm not sure if I'm in love.
5. I'm too young/old to get married.
6. I'm not ready to settle down.
7. I'll lose all my freedom.
8. I don't want to make a commitment until I have to.
9. I get scared when someone gets too close.

Some of the items on this list are reasonable concerns. However, others may be preventing you from finding what you want.

You may notice a pattern that all your relationships aren't working out for what appears to be the same reason. If you are unable to make changes on your own you may want to consider therapy. Therapy can help to highlight problematic patterns in relationships, explore the thoughts that create these feelings and figure out ways to improving how you handle relationships. Otherwise, you can go through life thinking you are just fine and everyone else is flawed or crazy in some way.

Adding to the anxiety of marriage are the cold, hard facts that half of all marriages end in divorce and ⅓ of those left married are unhappy. It is easy to see why there is so much hesitancy about getting married.

In spite of all the evidence that a lasting, fulfilling marriage is less than even money, people continue to go against the odds and get married. Most of us take the risk because the rewards can be well worth it. Even if we get close to the ideal of deep love, passion and fulfillment, these feelings create the most powerful, special experiences that we will have in life.

You probably don't need to be convinced about getting married because most people will end up married sooner or later. However, when you are in a situation where you begin to think about the possibility of marriage, there are some key factors that can help you ensure the best chance for success.

First, lets look at some of the reasons why people choose to get married.

1. I'm in love.
2. It's time to settle down.
3. My biological clock is ticking.
4. I don't want to end up alone.

5. S(he) makes me happy.

6. S(he) is rich.

7. The sex is great.

8. All my friends are married.

9. My parents are pressuring me.

10. I want to have a family.

11. S(he) makes me feel fulfilled and content.

12. The chemistry is great.

13. S(he) makes me laugh like no one else.

14. We have a lot in common.

15. We have so much fun even if we aren't doing anything.

16. I've never felt so much passion.

17. It just feels right.

18. I can't do any better.

19. S(he) gave me an ultimatum.

Some of these reasons are emotional and some are more practical. Some reasons may be conscious thoughts and you may be totally unaware of others. Whatever combination of factors fit your situation, everyone comes up with their own unique set of criteria for choosing who they want to spend the rest of their lives with. How many people can describe their criteria? Can they put their feelings into words? What do they consider more important: money and security or intimacy and passion?

When thinking about who you want to marry, it is crucial to know what you want and what your values are. If you know what's important to you, you'll know where to look. Does your current partner have all the things you are looking for?

Probably not. But does he or she have the qualities you must have and does he or she create the feelings that you must have in order to get married?

One helpful exercise to help identify your needs and values is to write down a list of all the qualities you would love to have in your partner. Sense of humor, warmth, integrity, loyalty, strength and sensitivity may be on your list. Next, write down all the feelings you want to experience with a partner before considering marriage. Passion, love, security, appreciation and fulfillment may make your list. These examples are just to get you going. You should be able to come up with 15–20 items for each list.

Next comes the tricky part. *There may be many intangible factors that cannot be easily described on paper.* Try to identify some of these intangibles by writing down several examples of what your potential partner did or said to create the feelings that you listed. For example, what makes you feel loved? Is it the way s(he) looks at you? Does your partner say just the right thing when you're sad? Whatever it is, write and example or two next to each item.

The final stage of the exercise is to highlight what you MUST HAVE in a relationship to consider marriage. Put a ** next to every quality and feeling that are absolutely necessary before you would consider marriage. These are the items you cannot do without. For example, sense of humor might be a necessity to you because laughing relaxes you. However, while you would love to be with someone who is philosophical, it is not a must to you. Does your current relationship have all the things you must have based on your list?

It is crucial to be able to sacrifice some of the things you would like to have in a relationship if all your necessities are in place. Don't put the pressure of having all your needs met exclusively by your relationship. If you aren't getting some of your needs met in your relationship, find them with a close friend or family member. Too many people get caught up in trying to find the perfect person. They often get excited in new relationships, but given time they can always find something wrong with their potential spouse. These people end relationships because they don't want to settle. Unfortunately, people get the wrong idea about settling. *Settling is doing without the things that you must have in a relationship. It is not about giving up things you might like to have but are not crucial to the long term success of the relationship.*

You have to take a serious look at yourself. If what you must have in a marriage is ridiculously rigid and unattainable you may very well end up lonely. Even if you find this idealized, "perfect" person (which is impossible) why should he/she pick you from all the other prospective suitors? *We tend to hold other people up to much higher standards than we do ourselves when it comes to relationships.* You may want somebody who is caring and selfless, yet you spend 99% of the day thinking about yourself.

The previous pages are a guide to help you sort out any of the confusion you may have about relationships and getting married. If you are certain you are in love and are clear about what you want and can give, the rest is easy—at least until you are married.

MARRIAGE

We all think about the dream marriage at one time or another. We think of contentment, fulfillment, love, intimacy, happiness and family. We hope that our spouse will be our soul mate, will bring out the best in us, will support us through hard times and will share the joys of life with us. If one is lucky enough to find a spouse that engenders most of these feelings, it is the most special type of relationship that life has to offer.

Everyone has their own unique set of conscious and unconscious set of criteria which create certain feelings and thoughts about their spouse. This is what we simply call "chemistry." However, the chemistry between spouses changes over time. Sometimes, the chemistry does not continue to mix after you've been married for several years. Conflict ensues. Read on and learn the **secrets of marriage**.

Physical Attractiveness

At the most basic level, lets take the oft used expression, "It was love at first sight." In more cynical terms this merely means you fell for your mate because of looks. No question that physical attractiveness draws you towards another person. You may even

55

tend to excuse some personality traits because of the way some-one looks. *However, one very important secret is NEVER decide to marry somebody based on how he or she looks.*

First of all, features change over time. People don't look the same way in their 50's as they did in their 20's. Looks fade, so if you get married because of how physically attracted you were to your partner, enjoy those first couple of years.

Second, even if by some miracle your partner's looks remain the same over time, the issue of physical attractiveness becomes much less of a factor in a marriage. After ten years, a man might appreciate a hot meal on a plate a lot more than his wife's curves. A woman is much more likely to appreciate some loving atten-tion a lot more than her husband's muscular body.

While attractiveness may fade on a purely physical level, it may improve over the course of a marriage on a more emotional level. A marriage based more on the physical than the emotional part is in trouble because physical attractiveness will fade over time. However, a marriage based on emotions and personality may make physical attractiveness last a lifetime. It may not be that your partner is objectively physically attractive but he or she becomes that way to you because of the emotional connection you have for him or her.

If you are lucky, you will be able to enjoy a great physical attraction in the short term and a deeper emotional connec-tion over the long term. Just don't be foolish enough to go for short term physical attractiveness over long term emotional attractiveness.

Sex

Most married couples have sex a couple times per week before children and a couple times per month after children. Put simply, the amount of sex declines over time. This is just part of human nature. You cannot have sex with the same person a thousand times and maintain the same desire that you had when you were early on in your relationship. You must have realistic expectations about your sex life in a marriage.

The secret with sex is to understand the stages that you will go through in your marriage. Most likely, the beginning stage (which you may have gone through before you got married) is filled with passionate, physical sex. You do it often and look forward to the experience with great anticipation.

Subtle, slow changes occur along the way and you notice that you are not looking forward to sex as much as you used to. The act is still fun, but the anticipation has diminished. You wonder if this is symbolic of your relationship in some way. You question where the passion has gone?

Most people just accept the state of affairs and lapse into the ½ hour twice a week routine. *The secret is to try and transition from passionate sex to loving sex.* Passion is purely physical but love is emotional. If your lovemaking reaches beyond the purely physical level, you can enjoy lasting good sex.

Women are much better than men with loving sex. They can derive a lot of pleasure from sexual experiences in a loving, committed relationship. Men have a lot of work to do in this area. They are more programmed for physical sex, and even when in a loving marriage, see sex as a more physical act than a woman does. Since this wears off after time, men need to learn to tap into their emotional feelings toward their wife during sex.

This is impossible if you are not in love any more and hard to do even when you still are in love.

Love

The key to sustaining physical attraction and good sex is being in love. Falling in love is easy. Staying in love is a lot harder. How do you remain in love with someone who you spend day after day and year after year with? How do maintain a fresh relationship when you know everything about each other already? How can you sustain the intensity of feelings when you have settled into a comfortable life routine? How can you possibly stay in love when you devote so little time to your relationship and so much time to you career, your children, paying the bills and keeping your home in order?

The sad but true answer is that you can't truly stay in love if you don't counteract the traps of life. The following secrets will allow you to move away from the chores you think you have to devote so much time to and towards building a better loving relationship.

Staying in love over 40 to 50 years means revising your expectations and goals of the relationship over time. For instance, when you first met your spouse, you most likely had a strong physical attraction, a lot of sex, good chemistry, great conversation and shared a lot of fun times. The intimacy that built from this contributed greatly to feeling "in love."

After the "honeymoon phase," your feelings probably started to change. The intensity of conversation diminished as you knew more and more about each other and you got caught up in your day to day life. Physical and sexual attraction reached its peak and you settled into more of a comfort zone. You spent more and more time relaxing at home and less time on going out "on dates." In short, the sense of the relationship being new and exciting wore off. This may change how you feel about your spouse. People often mistake a decrease in excitement as a decrease in love. Sometimes this may be the case. For the most part, however, people are just making the mistake of putting too narrow a definition on love.

Love is a lot more than lust, passion and excitement. If you see it that narrowly you won't stay in love for long. However, if you revise your expectations and feel love based on sharing your life together, common values, trust, compromise and thinking of your spouses needs as well as your own, you have a better chance of a successful marriage.

Of course, trust, commitment, loyalty, etc. are not the most exciting concepts in the world and they certainly contribute to different feelings of love than passion, excitement and sex. *Once the excitement phase of your marriage has passed, you better have other aspects that form the foundation of your relationship or your marriage is in big trouble.* Creating continuing love from trust, intimacy, commitment and loyalty is hard work but when you think about it, isn't a love based on virtues and values better than a love based on the shape of someone's ass?

Coming to Terms with Being Married

When the excitement phase of being married declines many people focus on what they are not getting in their marriage rather than what they are getting. Many people long to be a single again. They selectively remember the good things about being single. They fall into feeling "the grass is greener on the other side." Others may think that having kids as the answer.

Getting married is trading off one lifestyle for another. It is true that you lose out on certain things when you are married and have been with your spouse for several years. But why focus on what you are losing when you could be thinking about what you are gaining. For example, you may feel that you have lost some of your freedom to be spontaneous but you have also gained a partner to go out to dinner with every weekend. You may feel aggravated by your partner at times and may hate the inevitable fights but you will never feel lonely. If you are in trouble, your spouse is the first one to come through for you.

Meeting Needs in a Marriage

One of the most difficult things about being married is having to consider someone else's needs. You can't just think of yourself. This requires a lot of work because human nature programs you to think of yourself first. Hopefully, part of being in love is being able to consider your spouse's needs ahead of your own at times.

Even a simple thing such as listening to how your spouse's day went with interest goes a long way. Your spouse may have a need to vent and tell you about certain incidents that happened during the day. These incidents may seem unimportant to you but the act of listening for five minutes and putting off your need to do something else goes a long way.

Sacrificing some of your needs for your spouse's is a short term loss. He/she gets what he/she wants and you don't. Many times, sacrificing needs is not voluntary but part of a negotiation or argument. For example, it's important for your wife to spend a day with her family even though it means you have to miss the football game on Sunday. When your wife mentions that she wants to spend Sunday with her folks, you immediately balk and say you don't want to go. It's human nature to think of what you are missing. This does not make you selfish. If you are stubborn, however, an argument ensues which means someone is going to get their way and the other person will feel resentful. You resent going to her parents and she doesn't appreciate the fact that you're going because it was like pulling teeth just to get you to go.

The key to negotiating whose needs get met in a particular scenario is to try and forget about the running scorecard in your head about who is getting more of what they want in the relationship. Everyone thinks that they are the one getting taken advantage of by their spouse at some point. You have to have some faith that things will equal out over time.

How do get things to equal out? The first step is to be the one who gives first. Sacrifice some of your needs even if it goes against your nature. *The more you give, the more you will get back in return. If you are sacrificing your needs for your spouse voluntarily, your actions will be appreciated and reciprocated.* If you cook a nice dinner one night (even if you are tired from work) because you know your spouse will also be tired, you will have a lot of rewards. First of all, you will have the feeling of doing something nice for someone you love (giving). Second, you will most likely be met with some gratitude for your gestures (appreciation). Third, the person who received the gift will feel loved (caring). Fourth, you'll probably get a great meal yourself on a day that you're dead tired (reward). Then you will feel loved and cared about as well.

This is an example of a positive cycle that can be created just by sacrificing and giving a little. Both of you feel loved and appreciated and you've had two great meals. If on the other hand, you just think of your own needs and do nothing for your spouse, you will not feel loving, you will not be appreciated and you'll be having a lot of take out Chinese food.

If you are a giving partner in your relationship you will create a lot of love. If you are a taking partner you will create a lot of resentment. Furthermore, if you are a "taker," you will probably turn your spouse into a "taker" too.

This vicious cycle is one of the biggest reasons for divorce. One partner starts to feel that their needs are not being met, that they are being taken for granted and that they are not appreciated. Both partners sometimes feel the exact same way. Each tries to communicate their frustrations to the other without success. The frustration builds which leads to resentment. The resentment leads to acting selfishly. If you feel you are not getting what you need, you stop giving and start taking. *Once you start acting in your own self-interest without considering your spouse's needs, you can be certain that your spouse will start acting in exactly the same way.*

The end result is that the partners start acting like two self-interested individuals. The bond becomes fragile and instead of the partnership making each individual a better person, it makes each a worse person. Instead of making the combined marriage unit stronger, it becomes weaker. Once a marriage reaches this stage, it is only a matter of time before one partner does or says something that cannot be forgiven and the road to divorce or an unhappy marriage has begun.

The simplest way to avoid this unpleasant outcome is to start giving a little bit more in your relationship. Think about your spouse in an altruistic fashion. When your altruism is reciprocated, show some appreciation and gratitude toward your spouse. Inevitably, your spouse will start acting the same way and you'll have a great marriage. If your spouse takes advantage of your continued kindness and giving on a consistent basis and does not reciprocate then you have problems, but at least you know you did your part to try and make the relationship the best it could possibly be.

Expectations

One of the biggest stumbling blocks to a long marriage is the false expectations created about what a happy marriage is. Listed below are some of these false expectations which create a tremendous amount of disappointment and disillusionment with marriage.

1. "My spouse is not attractive as she used to be when we first got married." This is usually a bigger problem for men who often complain about issues such as weight gain and aging. Well, what did you expect? Did you think your wife could maintain a 25 year old body when she's 45? The secret is to acknowledge that looks change with age and usually for the worse. If your spouse's appearance stays the same or gets better with age, consider it a pleasant surprise, but don't make it an expectation.

2. "My spouse does not pay as much attention to me as he/she used to." Why should this be an expectation when chances are that work and family obligations have become increasing pressures in your lives. Whether it is raising kids and/or working longer hours at the office to maintain the type of lifestyle that you want, you will have to sacrifice something—especially if you are so tired at the end of the day that you can't do anything but watch TV. The key here is not to expect the same amount of attention or, if you

want more attention, to change your life goals so the relationship becomes more of a priority.

3. "We don't have the same passion for each other as we used to." Why should you? You see each other day after day, year after year, unshaven, unshowered and at your worst moments. The illusion of the perfect spouse is broken one way or another. You should not expect passion to be everlasting. However, you can hope for moments of passion in your marriage. Whether it be a sexual experience, an intimate conversation or a romantic vacation, the passion can still be rekindled. Enjoy these moments and look forward to them but do not try to convince yourself that your marriage is in trouble due to a decrease is in passion.

4. "We never have enough money to do the things we want." Many people go into a marriage expecting a comfortable lifestyle financially. However, in most cases you underestimate how much life costs. You end up in a less than perfect house, you can't go to the French Riviera every summer and you have to work 50 or more hours per week just to be able to live a middle class lifestyle with moderate savings.

    Both spouses need to go into a marriage thinking realistically about the financial possibilities. If you don't, you may end up resenting your situation. One spouse will be angry at the other for spending too much money. One spouse feels the other doesn't work hard enough or contribute enough financially. You both get caught up in comparing your situations to your friends and neighbors. The Smith's have a Cadillac and we drive a Ford. Too much energy in the marriage becomes devoted to the almighty dollar. If you have a realistic expectation of your situation, you can both be extremely happy because money is not the most important thing in the relationship.

5. "Things will get better when we have a family." This can be true because kids are usually a great joy to parents. However, they can also be the greatest source of stress and strain in the relationship. Don't look to children to make up for what's missing in your relationship. To be the best parents, you'll need to have worked through your marriage issues first. Don't expect that kids will make your marriage stronger. Having children is not about what they can do for your you. It's about what you can do for them.

6. "My spouse is not meeting all of my needs." Many people mistakenly expect that their spouse has to be the only one to fulfill your needs. This is asking too much from any one person. If you love shopping, find a friend with this interest if your spouse hates to go. People have a lot of needs and need to get them filled by friends, hobbies and family, not just their spouse. If you look to get what you want from a variety of sources, you'll put a lot less pressure on the marriage. You'll feel satisfaction when you are getting what you need in your marriage and not feel disappointed when you're not getting something because you can always get it somewhere else. You should only expect you spouse to fulfill your major needs most of the time and hopefully you are doing the same for your spouse.

Divorce

If you follow the suggestions of the past several chapters, your marriage will most likely not come to divorce. However, if it has reached that point and there is no turning back there are several methods to ease the pain of the separation.

First of all, if you had a pre-nuptual agreement, the financial picture will be a lot better. In most cases, this was not considered as both members decided there was no way they were ever going to get divorced and a pre-nup meant a lack of trust and faith in the relationship. However, a couple should look at the pre-nup like an insurance policy. You buy life insurance and you don't want to die. Similarly, you can have a pre-nup and not think you'll get divorced.

If you're past this option and you are in the midst of a bitter divorce, its best to consider all savings and assets gone. Either your spouse will get it or the blood sucking lawyers will, but either way it's gone. If you waste your time and energy fighting for every last penny, you'll be miserable. At worst, you'll get nothing and have to begin anew. But remember, if you're employed and living on your own, you'll be pleasantly surprised at how fast you can save up some money.

The financial picture becomes a little more cloudy when you have to pay or are receiving child support payments. Depending on what side you're on, it's never enough or it's too much.

The whole divorce picture is lousy when kids are involved. The bright side is that kids don't have to be subjected to your unworkable relationship. See the Children chapter for some tips on how to manage a divorce when you have children.

Conclusions

Marriage is not the solution to finding a happy life. It can be, however, a step in the right direction. The biggest step to finding happiness in marriage is how hard you are willing to work at it. The institution of marriage is wrought with hurdles and problems. You don't always get what you want. You have to consider another person's feelings at the expense of your own at times. You have to be willing to sacrifice a lot when you get married. However, if you work hard at it and try to implement some of the suggestions from this chapter, chances are pretty good that you can make a life for you and your spouse that fulfills most of what you were looking for when you got married in the first place.

CHILDREN

There is no blueprint for raising children. No matter what you do as a parent, there will always be problems. The key is how you handle these problems. How you handle either the common every day problems of raising children or the unexpected crises depends on your parenting style. The following is a short description of the most common parenting styles.

Parenting Styles

As an example, let's say a child stops doing her homework. A parent that is **uninvolved** may not know or care that a problem exists. Every once in a while they ask their child how they are doing in school and the kid says "OK." A bad report card comes and the parent explodes for a day and then forgets about it.

Compare this to the overly **permissive parent**. In the same situation, the child comes home with a bad report card and vows to do better next time. There are no consequences and the child learns how easy it is to con his or her parent. With the permissive parent, there is always a next time. The kids get away with just about anything.

At the other extreme is the **disciplinarian drill sergeant** parent. This parent is on top of the children in every area. They will almost certainly know that their child is not doing homework and the child will be punished accordingly. As a matter of fact, a child in this family will NEVER be allowed to miss homework. If it's a choice between the Super Bowl and math homework, the kids will have to do the math. There are strict rules with very little flexibility or understanding. This parent may have trouble showing caring or warmth. The child feels he or she is in boot camp.

The best parenting style is one that combines authority and discipline with love and understanding. It's okay to punish a child for a bad report card or for not doing homework, but also try to find out if everything is okay. Have rules in the home but allow for some flexibility. If you have an 11:00 P.M. curfew on weekends and the child wants to go to an event where they won't get home until 12:00 A.M., show some understanding. Many parents intuitively understand this delicate balance.

However, many others don't get it. They think they are strict because they yell at their child and punish them harshly (disciplinarian), but meanwhile they don't even know half the trouble the child gets into (uninvolved).

Furthermore, if you ask a parent about their style of parenting, they often have very little awareness. No one classifies themselves as an uninvolved parent. Very few will admit to being overly permissive. Some will say they are overly strict but it's for the child's own good.

What Qualities Do Parents Need To Raise Children Successfully?

Herein lies one of the biggest problems of parenting. Every parent seems to feel that they are just the right blend of disciplinarian, caregiver, coach, and role model. Few people ever think they are not a great parent. If you are a parent reading this next section, take a look in the mirror and see if you are really doing what it takes to raise a happy, well adjusted child.

The first secret to children is that 95% of their problems are a response to their parents' problems. A child does not become angry and misbehave out of nowhere. Kids don't become withdrawn and depressed without good reason. If parents can address their own problems, it is almost guaranteed that their kid's problems will improve as well.

You have the best chance of successfully raising a child if you:

1. show affection and express love.
2. are responsive to your children's needs.
3. encourage the children to do well but don't push to hard.
4. are available every day to help, provide consistency and supervision.
5. teach values and serve as a role model for those values.

Love and Affection

All parents love their kids but some have strange ways of showing it. Unconditional love is one of the greatest gifts a parent can give to a child. It is one of the main building blocks of self-esteem and confidence in kids. It is easier for children who are loved to feel good about themselves.

A parent should never assume their kids feel loved. They need to be shown love. If you are not involved with your kids because of "other life priorities," your children will start to feel unimportant and perhaps unloved. Time equals love to some degree, but how you spend the time is even more crucial.

When you are with your child, it is important to show affection. This may not be natural for some parents. Don't worry. Children can bring out affection in even the most stoic people.

Responsive to Child's Needs

You wouldn't believe how often parents feel they are being responsive to their child's needs when they are really thinking more about themselves. When you push your child to excel in school at the expense of a social life and extra curricular activities, is this in the best interest of the child? When your child brings home a 90 average and your response is "you'll have to do better than that to get into an Ivy League school," what tone do you think this sets for your child?

Perhaps part of your motivation is so you can brag to your friends that your child is going to an Ivy League college. Perhaps you think that the road to happiness for your child is academic and professional success. However, are you really being responsive to your child's needs? If the child wants to spend eight hours a day studying and has a passion for academics, you would be being responsive to your child if you assisted them in achieving these goals. However, if your child wants to spend time with friends and play some touch football, and is happy to maintain a "B" average, isn't this okay? Any parent who would push this child to get A's under the guise that the child doesn't know what is good for him is misguided.

Let's say your child succeeds academically despite the parental pressure and goes on to become a lawyer. Is this best for the child? The child may make a lot of money but be miserable. Second of all, the parent may have unintentionally instilled an attitude in the now grown child that success is only measured by achievement and accomplishment. Relaxing and spending time with family become secondary to success. Is this really what you wanted for your child?

Tips for being responsive:

1. Each child must be allowed to develop his or her own unique talents. Parents should never push their children to pursue what the parent may have missed out on. For example, the ex-jock parent should not push their child to do whatever it takes to make the pros if it is not the child's passion as well.

2. Make sure you have kids when you are ready to think of your child before yourself. You don't have kids because of what they can do for you. It's about what you can do for them.

Encouraging Your Child to Succeed

Many parents think they are being encouraging but are actually pressuring and pushing their children. Encouraging means to help your children pursue their goals. It means being there to build them back up after a disappointment. It means motivating them to try their best in areas of their choosing. It means rewarding effort more than success.

Remember that encouragement builds confidence, but pressuring and pushing saps confidence. Reward efforts more than results. If the child is a hardworking "A" student who brings home a "B" one day, be sure to say that they are doing great and that one "B" is not going to kill him or her.

Let's say your daughter is interested in playing the piano. She chooses to practice an hour a day. In high school, she decides to enter a competition where she really has a good chance of winning a music school scholarship. She ends up having a bad day and does not win the scholarship or any award. As a parent do you:

A. feel bad for her?

B. feel disappointed in her?

C. tell her she has to practice harder if she wants to win?

D. tell her that piano isn't a future career option anyway?

E. tell her that she's a great pianist who just had a bad day, and her day will come sooner or later if she keeps on trying her best?

Hopefully, you answered A and E. This is how you should feel for your child and one good way to encourage them through a major disappointment.

Availability

In the past several years, we have become a society where both parents are often working full time. One or both parents may be working as long as 60–70 hours a week. It is becoming far less common for children to have full time parents. Finances play a major role in this unfortunate circumstance. However, it is crucial for one or both parents to scale back on their workloads and concentrate on being parents when raising a child. Even if this requires a sacrifice in lifestyle for a few years, being available for an impressionable young child is more important. It would be a huge mistake to leave those all important daytime hours to a nanny or baby-sitter. As qualified as the nanny may be, he or she is not your child's parent.

One secret is to set up a savings account before you have children. Then it may be feasible for one parent to take a year off from work or at least cut back on his or her hours. It's crucial for both parents to have time to spend with their new born child. A child savings account may give you this time.

You may even need to plan several years ahead. The prosperity chapter can give you the techniques to save money. Plan long and hard for parenthood. You may have to buy a less expensive house and put cash away for your future family. *Start a child fund at least 3–5 years before having children if you have limited savings.* Put away a fixed amount every month so you'll have a nest egg. The way the world works, having extra money can buy you time to be with your child. Nothing is more valuable.

Fathers often fall into the trap of working harder and being less available at home after having a child. The common misperception is that mothers are crucial to a child's development and fathers are not. Thus, mothers often cut back on work and fathers work more. They get home at 7:00 P.M., eat dinner, play with their kid for a little while and then drop off to sleep exhausted from the long day.

At the other extreme, some mothers often fall into the trap of spending all their time with their baby. They stop working, spend very little time with friends and lose the social network that they created for themselves before they had children. Feelings of loneliness, isolation and boredom start to creep into their lives.

Balance is the key for both parents. Each partnership should find whatever balance works for them but don't fall into the extremes. Set up a lifestyle so that both of you can spend lots of time with your children.

Teaching Values

The best way to teach proper values to your children is to practice what you preach. If you value education, go to parent/teacher meetings when invited. Take an interest in your child's schooling. Find out what they did in school each day. Parents who say "you have to do good in school" to their kids but then never see if the child is "doing good" are not really teaching the value of education to a child.

As another example, let's say parents value integrity. How can you instill this value to your child? You must act as the role model for integrity. Apologize if you have made a mistake. If you see someone in need, go out of your way to help. Even if you see that doing something underhanded will get you ahead faster, take the virtuous route. *Remember that your children are watching your behavior and taking cues how to act themselves.*

When children observe their parents arguing, they are learning how to resolve disputes themselves. If the parents resort to acting irrationally, cursing, screaming and/or physical battering, the children experience that this is the way that people deal with anger. Even though kids may understand that it is wrong to act in this way, their parents' behavior seeps into their consciousness and becomes a part of their personality whether they like it or not. Think about certain things you did not like about how your parents raised you. After you are a parent yourself, try to see how much you end up acting like your own parents.

The old saying "the apple doesn't fall far from the tree" often holds true.

The biggest problem with acting like a role model for your children is that most people think everything they do is right. If they explode in anger, they were provoked and had a good reason to get angry. If they rip someone off financially, they feel that it is okay because this is the way of the world. *One of the secrets of parenting is to be able to look at yourself with a self-critical eye.* If your spouse, friend, co-worker or child gives you feedback about the way you do things, think about what they say. Look at the issue from someone else's point of view.

Adolescence

This is a very tricky time for even the most accomplished of parents. Your kids are heading towards a time where their own opinions and those of their friends matters a lot more then parental advice. The biggest secret for parents of adolescents is to accept that your kids are growing up and allow them some slack so that they can make mistakes. It is also crucial to provide a sturdy, safe, predictable environment at home since your adolescent's emotional life is far from predictable.

Also, you must continue to build upon the values you taught your kid through childhood. The difference in adolescence is that your child is going to develop his or her own value system. They are reaching an age when you cannot impose your values on them. If you are adamant against using drugs, don't be surprised if your child experiments a little bit. It would be only natural for the curious adolescent to see for himself what the big deal is and why his parents are so against drugs. Experience may teach the youngster that his parents are right about drugs.

However, the adolescent may also decide to adopt a less extreme policy about drugs. Wouldn't you be glad if you were a parent that had also taught your child responsibility, judgment and the ability to look at the consequences of his or her actions? You can't police your adolescent son or daughter all the time, but you can prevent a lot of trouble by raising them well.

Here's a typical example of drinking and adolescence. Let's say your 17 year old son had a few too many at a party. He knows you are against drinking. He knows you will be disappointed in him if you find out. Thus, instead of calling you for a ride at 2:00 A.M. because no one is sober enough to drive, he decides to get a ride with a drunken friend hoping he can sneak in the house unnoticed late at night. The boy is weighing the dangers of drunk driving versus disappointed, angry, judgmental parents. Adolescents tend to hide things from their parents because they are afraid of disappointing them. Fear of embarrassment, humiliation, and guilt lead to lies and omissions from time to time. If you are an overly judgmental parent, you can be sure that the lies may go further than "I think I'm running a temperature and can't go to school today."

How about sex? As a parent, I'm sure you have strong beliefs on this issue and your morals for your children are probably more stringent than what you did yourself at their age. Do you forbid your son or daughter to have sex? Do you adopt a "don't ask, don't tell" policy? *Another of the secrets of raising a child is that parents need to think in terms of prevention, not just putting out fires when they occur.* You must make your kids aware of the risks and safeguards of sex. Be available to talk about sex with your kids but don't force the issue. As horrifying as it is for you to think that your 16 year old daughter might be sexually active, it is just as horrifying for your daughter to have to ask you about sex education.

Whatever the issue, whether it be school, sex, drugs or rock and roll, remember that your adolescent child is developing their own unique identity and belief system. Accept some rebellion as part of the process. Most adolescents will take some risks. It is impossible for a parent to attempt to control everything. You can't be overprotective or too controlling. You can, however, instill a set of values that your kids can use for a lifetime. You can't influence particular situations but you can influence your children's beliefs about right and wrong, as well as their views about integrity.

The bottom line is that your children will not always listen to you. Even if they know you are right, they need to find out for themselves. If you're lucky, they will learn from their experience and also have a good memory for what you have tried to teach them along the way. Mark Twain once said, "I can't believe how much my parents learned between my ages 16 and 21."

Divorce and Children

Single parent homes can be very successful. Often, both child and parent will be relieved after a divorce due to the reduced tension in the household. The best tips for a parent who is in the midst of a divorce are:

1. Make sure your child does not feel like he or she is to blame.

2. Don't put your child in the middle of your marital tension.

3. Provide a stable and secure home environment.

4. Allow the children to be loved by both parents. Make sure both parents are involved.

5. If step-parents become an issue, make sure you discuss the parameters of the relationship with both your new partner and your child. Step-parents are not all wicked like they were in Cinderella. A big brother/big sister type of relationship can be important to a child. Never try to replace the child's biological parent.

Fatherhood

The most important secret for fathers is to set up your life so that you can spend time with your children. A very common problem for fathers is that they leave most of the child raising to the child's mother. For example, when there is a parent-teacher conference at school, only mom shows up 90% of the time. Usually, mom helps the child with their homework after school. Mom drives the kids to and from soccer practice and roots the kids on during their games.

To be an available father, you need to manage your time so that you can get away from the office every once in a while on a weekday afternoon so you can spend quality time with your kids and be involved in their day to day experiences. Usually, this means keeping a reasonable work schedule. Unfortunately, many fathers get stuck in a Catch-22 situation. When the kids are born, you need more cash. Thus, you spend more time working and less time with the kids.

Do not fall into the trap of becoming the ox in the field. You are not the sole provider for the family. Your wife may insist your new baby needs a state of the art baby carriage. This does not necessarily mean that you have to work extra hours to be able to afford it. Discuss financial issues with your wife and come up with an equitable and fair solution for savings and spending. For example, agree with her that it is important that your child have the best things that you can afford. Pose the question of what sacrifices each of you will need to make to be able to afford anything that is a little out of your reach.

Motherhood

The most important secret for mothers is to try and maintain a balanced life after having children. Mothers have a strong pull toward nurturance. Often, this means not seeing friends and not going back to work. This can set up a life which is very isolating. Many new mothers fall into the trap of setting up a lifestyle where they do not have any fun with other adults. If they do go out, it's only with someone else who has a baby or at the very least, the baby comes along on every social occasion. This ultimately means that the baby will be the center of attention. All of your energy is geared toward care taking.

Do not fall into the trap of only being a caregiver and meeting the needs of your baby without having your own needs met. This means seeing friends once in a while and leaving the baby with a sitter. It means going out to dinner with your husband without constantly having to call home to see how the baby is doing. It means being able to separate from your child. The subject of separation is usually written about kids trying to separate from parents. However, this works both ways. *A woman's identity is not solely being a mother to a child.* Try to manage a life where you can be a mother, wife, employee, and friend. The more balance you can achieve, the better off you will be and the better off your child will be as well. Serving as a role model is one of the most important functions you serve as a parent. Imagine having a daughter who sees that her mother is always there for her, but also has a successful marriage and a satisfying career.

Raising children is not easy. However, the better you are able to manage the day to day issues inherent in raising your kids, the better life will be for both you and your children.

PROSPERITY

What does prosperity mean to you? You might say I want a million dollars in cash, a new Lexus and a four bedroom home. Would it really take all that to make you prosperous? Why do you want all these lavish material possessions? Would such wealth bring you true happiness?

How can you become extremely wealthy in the 21st century? Is it worth the sacrifice and effort? Can you get rich quick? The following chapter will help you find answers to these intriguing questions. You will lean the secret of life known as **prosperity**.

THE TEN MYTHS OF MONEY

1. **Money Is the Root of All Evil**—We're willing to wager that you've known some evil people of all economic standings. Greed leads to many evil pursuits, but so does jealousy, anger and many other human frailties.

2. **Money Can't Buy You Love**—While there is some truth in this statement, it isn't completely accurate. Money can give you increased opportunities to find love. How many

wealthy people can't get a date? Money is a powerful aphrodisiac.

3. **Money Would Relieve Me of My Worries**—In most cases, money causes more worries. Once you have it, you are obsessed with keeping every cent. It is much easier to get a poor man to buy you a drink than a rich one. A wealthy person is usually constantly worried about a stock market crash, thieves and conniving relatives. A middle class person comes home from work at 5:00 and relaxes. A wealthy person may work until 9:00, then worry and scheme for the rest of the evening.

4. **If I Were Rich, I'd Have More Free Time**—If you are like most wealthy people, you'd have less free time. You would have much greater responsibilities and a more extensive workload. If you make a million dollars a year, you may hesitate to take a month off because it would cost you almost $100,000. Instead you would probably choose to work constantly to keep the cash flowing.

5. **If I Were Rich, I'd Be a Nicer Person**—Money usually makes you more of whatever you already are. If you are generous, you'll become more generous. If you are mean, you'll become more mean.

6. **If I Were Wealthy, People Would like Me More**— Unfortunately, people are a jealous lot. Most people would be kind to you in person, and then talk about you behind your back. It would be next to impossible to know who your true friends were.

7. **If I Were Rich, I'd Have Less Problems**—Wealth brings with it a whole new set of problems. Lawsuits and IRS audits are just two of the major headaches you'll face. You'll be surprised to learn how many people are eager to separate you from your new found wealth.

8. **I'd Be More Secure with More Money**—While there is some truth in this statement, it ignores a major security issue, CRIME. The world is riddled with thieves who want to turn your riches into their ill-gotten gains. Protecting your assets from theft is a major new concern.

9. **The Best Things in Life Are Free**—I guess it depends on what you enjoy. Taking your children to Disney World, eating lobsters and buying a new outfit all take cash.

10. **If I Had More Money I'd Be Happy and Content**—While you would be able to afford more luxurious items, you won't necessarily become a happier person. A miserable person will find a way to stay miserable even with a million dollars and a happy person can remain content with just a few dollars.

Once you come to terms with the "myths of money" you are in a better position to judge what it means to be prosperous. Prosperity is not about working 90 hours a week, accumulating cash and never seeing your family. *Prosperity is having enough resources to meet your financial needs, being able to buy what you want and having the free time to enjoy life.*

Of course, the amount of resources you want and the free time that you need are up to you. If you decide you want to be wealthy through starting your own business, you must be prepared to take big financial risks and work hard for years. It requires patience and perseverance. If you decide you want wealth through working in a lucrative industry, be prepared to be very patient before you get to the top. You're not going to become partner in a law firm right after law school. You're probably going to have to put in 70 hour weeks for a couple of years just to be considered for partner.

Don't make the mistake of thinking you'll get rich quick. It is possible but you'll have to take enormous risks that have a very poor chance of success. For example, you may decide to invest lots of money in the newest, cutting edge technology stocks. You've read all the stories about how if you had bought Cisco in 1990 you would be a multi-millionaire now. For every Cisco, there are hundreds of technology stocks that are now bankrupt.

If you are prepared to make the necessary sacrifices to become wealthy, you must examine why you want the money. You may say I want my own jet. Do you really have a strong desire for personal aviation or do you want to show off for all your friends and relatives? Maybe you would like to become rich for competitive reasons. Maybe you feel money is life's report card. There is nothing wrong with this philosophy if it gives you a reason to spring out of bed in the morning. However, remember whoever dies with the most toys still dies. It's all relative. No matter how much money you accumulate, there will always be those wealthier. You can never really win the game. *At the end of your life, your wealth is not going to be as important to you as the kind of person you've become.* If you like what you see when you look in the mirror, and you feel your life has made the world a better place, you'll have wealth beyond your wildest dreams.

You may think these ideas are preposterous. Money is wonderful. Money is fantastic. We want you to have all material possessions you desire. We're simply pointing out that money doesn't guarantee happiness. However, wealth does offer advantages if you make a commitment to making money.

TOP TEN WAYS THAT MONEY BUYS HAPPINESS

1. **The Luxuries of Life**—If you have the means, you can afford the little "extras" in life. Your level of comfort can be improved. Designer underwear fits a little better and can put you in a nicer mood. You can spend more on food and improve the quality of your meals. You can go to a movie or a concert, enjoy an $80 bottle of wine, take a vacation to Australia, drive a luxury car and have a home filled with your favorite things without breaking your budget.

2. **Better Life for Your Children**—Everyone wishes their children an easier life than they had. You don't want your children to suffer like you did. Unfortunately, its a "Catch-22" because out of this suffering emerges character. Still, with money and connections, you can pave the way for your children to have an easier life.

3. **Bouncing Back from Setbacks**—"Into everyone's life a little rain must fall." Unfortunately, sometimes that rain is a hurricane. You may suffer a financial disaster. A long bout with illness, unemployment, a flood or a burglary are just a few of the possible monetary pitfalls of life. These circumstances afflict both the rich and poor. The difference is that the rich are better able to weather the calamity and mount a comeback.

4. **Medical Care**—The ruinous cost of medical care destroys many lives. Prescriptions are very expensive and often not covered by insurance. Many unfortunate people must decide, for example, between their blood pressure and diabetes drugs each month. Even if you are lucky enough to have good insurance, the deductibles and the percentage not covered can add up to thousands of dollars.

The wealthy have a great advantage over others obtaining the limited resources of medical care.

5. **Flexibility in Business**—One of the saddest facts of life is that so many people say "Thank God its Friday" or "I hate Mondays." Life is of limited duration. It's a terrible personal tragedy to be stuck in a job you absolutely hate, but many people have no choice because they don't have the capital resources to make a change. Without wealth, an individual is working without a safety net and can't afford to take any risks.

6. **You Don't Have to Live on Anyone's Largess**—If you have financial resources, you can live independently. You probably can count on less people than you think. Hopefully, you will never become destitute and have to find out who your friends really are. Even if you have people you can count on, maybe you are the kind of person who doesn't like to receive charity. If you have wealth, you'll remain financially independent.

7. **Education**—The only thing more expensive in the United States than medical care is education. The costs are absolutely ridiculous. Public schools are just as costly as private ones, except a portion of the fee is picked up by the government. Advanced degrees are almost compulsory in this day and age, so that means even more money is necessary to complete the educational process.

8. **Travel**—Travel is one of life's greatest pleasures. Adventures in foreign lands are memorable experiences. Unfortunately, without cash you better get used to home sweet home.

9. **Stronger Relationships**—Many marriages break up because of financial problems. The stresses of normal life are multiplied by money pressures. Money can't buy happiness, but it can buy security. Security is great for a marriage.

10. **Making a Difference**—The last but not least reason money buys happiness is that you can make a difference in other people's lives. You can't help the poor by becoming one of them. You may find that helping others gives you a joy that can't be matched by a material possession.

Making Money

The best way to achieve a high income is to develop a marketable skill. The more rare and marketable the skill, the higher the income. Do you ever wonder why professional athletes are paid so much money? It is because only several hundred people in the world can do what they do. If you can become an expert in a valued field, you will have huge earning potential. It doesn't matter whether you are a doctor, plumber or salesperson. A high income is guaranteed. Once established in a field, you can hire others to work for you and take advantage of leverage. People will actually make money for you.

There is both risk and aggravation if you start your own business. Most businesses fail in the first year. If successful, however, your business can be financially and personally rewarding. The "Career" chapter will give you helpful hints on how to establish your own business. The point here is that it can be a source of high income.

A more reliable and less risky source of high income is employment with a large company. If you developed a marketable skill in sales for example, apply for a job with a successful corporation. Larger companies pay more than their smaller rivals. Successful salespeople in large companies often bring in more than $100,000 a year. You may already be employed with a large organization. If so, you must find a way to bring value to your company. Develop a skill than most other employees in the company don't have. You will be compensated well for your expertise. *The more money you can make for them, the more money they will give to you.*

If you want to become wealthy, you will also have to work in a financially profitable field. This is one of the sacrifices you'll need to make for riches. Social work and teaching are noble endeavors but not financially lucrative. You are the only one who can decide if money is a potent enough motivation to excite you about work every day.

Is it worth the time, effort and sacrifice to accumulate wealth? Before you lies the information you need to come to you own conclusion. Whether you decide you want to be wealthy or just financially comfortable, use the upcoming sections on making, saving and investing money as your guide. Your path to financial security entails the following:

1. You must spend less than you make
2. You must wisely invest the difference
3. You must re-invest the profits and dividends
4. You must protect your assets

Saving Money

Without budgeting, you have no chance to accumulate riches. How often have you read in the paper or seen on TV that superstar athletes and actors have gone bankrupt? MC Hammer and Burt Reynolds are just two examples.

There is a basic law of the universe that interferes with people's financial well being. *Your expenses swell to meet your income.* Have you noticed as the years have gone by your income has increased but it is just as hard as ever to save money. Also, you don't seem to be living that much better than you did when your income was half as much. You must look at how you are managing your assets and expenses.

Start a budget. The key to budgeting is writing it down. In putting a budget on paper you are setting concrete goals. If you do not put it on paper, you may let your expenses get out of hand.

THE SIX STEPS TO BUDGETARY SUCCESS

1. Write down everything you spend for an entire month. Do not try to control your spending. Live as you normally do but write down all your expenses. Look at your credit card bill at the end of the month. If you are like most people, you will be horrified when you see how you squander away your hard earned income.

2. Write down all sources of after tax income per month. This allows you to know exactly what money you have to work with each month.

3. Write down all expenses. This includes fixed expenses and miscellaneous items. Don't forget to allow for things like car repair and entertainment expenses. By examining the work you did in Step 1, you should be able to figure out what expenses you have each month.

4. See where you can cut your expenses. The best way to cut fat out of a budget is to lower your major costs. Do you really need to drive a new car? If you do, you are a victim of finance and high insurance premiums. The cost of this indulgence over a lifetime is absolutely incredible. If you pay cash for a reliable used car, you are saving yourself

about $600 a month. If you invested that $600 a month, even at an average rate of return for 25 years, you would net over $700,000. You might ask yourself, "Is the admiration I receive from my friends and co-workers for my new vehicle worth three quarters of a million dollars?" If the answer is no, buy reliable used cars from now on and transfer this savings to your bottom line.

5. Another way to save money is by limiting the use of credit card purchases. If you can't pay your bill in full each month, you aren't budgeting correctly. If you do use your credit card, make sure you pay it off in full each month. Interest rates on credit cards are usurious, often up to 20%. Also, it is a lot easier to make an impulse purchase by putting it on "fantastic plastic" than by counting out the cash to the clerk. Many people are so burdened by credit card debt that they have virtually no chance of accumulating wealth, no matter how high their income.

6. The last and most important step to budgetary success is to keep your eyes on the prize. You must be focused squarely on your goal to attain financial security and/or wealth. If you don't budget, you will never save money to invest no matter what your income might be. Building wealth means putting off immediate gratification. Don't buy the leather couch now and you might be able to buy 15 down the road.

Investment

Once you have secured an income and budgeted to achieve a surplus where should you invest the difference? Here are the best options.

1. **Stocks**—Stocks represent an equity interest in a company. Over time, a stock's price rises in relation to the company's earnings. In the short term, stocks rise and fall on emotion and the general market is virtually impossible to predict. Historically, diversified investments in stocks can offer you a 10% annual gain over the long term (more than 5 years). While the market fluctuates up and down in the short term, it has been the best place to invest your money if you have a long term approach.

2. **Mutual Funds**—Many people these days like to invest through mutual funds. Mutual funds are companies that offer an investment in stocks and bonds for a small management fee. Mutual funds are an excellent source of diversification. By investing in a fund, you are actually investing in the fund's portfolio of stocks and bonds.

3. **Bonds**—The advantage of bonds is that they offer you a fixed rate of return (anywhere from 4–8% annually). You are not going to suffer in a down stock market. You know exactly how much money you will have from year to year. The disadvantage of bonds is that they do not give you as high a return as long term stock or mutual fund investing.

How you invest your money (stocks, mutual funds and/or bonds) depends on your age, tolerance for risk and long term goals. While a financial advisor can help you sort this out, it is better to learn investing for yourself. For every honest advisor, there is another ready to rip you off. To save you the time and trouble of researching investing yourself, we provide you with the best possible investment strategy. Master the following principles and you will achieve the **secrets of prosperity**.

NINE STEPS TO INVESTMENT SUCCESS

1. **Retirement**—Make sure you secure your future. This is the first and foremost step to assuring financial well being. Retirement money is gained through several sources: Social Security, 401k or equivalent retirement program, IRA savings and personal savings. *If your company offers a 401k or other retirement program, elect to deduct the maximum from your check each pay period.* Companies will often match this amount. Even if they don't, this money is tax deferred. You may also be able to open an individual retirement account (IRA) in addition to your retirement plan at work. The new Roth IRA allows you to invest without having to pay taxes when you eventually withdraw the money. 401k or IRA savings *grows tax deferred and uses the miracle of compound interest. You accumulate savings at an exceptional rate. It is possible for many people to achieve a million dollar nest egg simply by fully funding their retirement plan.* As an example, Mr. B, a teacher, fully funded his 401k from age 25 to retirement at 57. The approximately $10,000 per year grew to a million even though only $300,000 was invested over all.

2. **Where to Put Your Money**—Invest in index mutual funds. Index funds are passively managed and very tax efficient. They do not have the large turnover of actively managed funds and have very limited capital gains distributions. The income tax is therefore deferred for the most part until you sell the fund, perhaps many decades later. Actively managed funds incur high expense ratios and are forced to distribute regular capital gains. You are taxed each year on this capital gains distribution. As we discussed above in step one, tax deferred growth can be the key to accumulating wealth. The most common index is the U.S. S&P 500.

This represents the 500 largest companies in the United States and makes up over 70% of the total market capitalization of the stock market. *An S&P Index Fund does better than 90% of all mutual funds over the long term.* Some sectors of the stock market always outperform the general market. It is impossible to determine which group will be hot in advance. For example, semiconductor stocks may be up 50% versus 10% for the S&P in one random year. You may be tempted to sell your index position and transfer your assets to the sizzling semiconductor stocks. Do not make this mistake. Besides ruining the tax benefits of your index investments, you probably would enter the semiconductor rally at the wrong time. Do not let greed get the better of you. *Remember, it is hard to get rich quick but easy to get rich slowly.* You will be able to achieve a 10% annual gain over the long term with index fund investing. While this may not seem like a lot, it means *you'll double your money every seven years.* Most major mutual fund companies offer a fund that matches the performance of the S&P 500.

3. **Don't Trust Stock Brokers**—The exception to this rule is if you have a trusted friend or relative in the business. Many stockbrokers will have you move in and out of stocks and mutual funds which generate nothing but capital gains taxes for you. However, they'll make hefty commissions for themselves. Like a car mechanic, if you can find a trusted broker they are worth their weight in gold. It's best, however, to learn to make your own investment decisions.

4. **Dollar Cost Averaging**—This may sound like a fancy term but is the best way to save money and invest at the same time. Basically, dollar cost averaging means that you

invest a fixed amount into a stock or fund monthly or quarterly. You do not try to time the market. Lets say that you can invest $100 dollars per month in your index fund. When the market is down, you buy more because your $100 can get you more shares. When the market is high, you buy less. If your index fund is $30 dollars a share on a particular month, you can get three shares. If it's $50 per a share, you can get two shares. Since the price of your index fund will invariably go up long term, you will have bought many of your shares "on sale." You can also dollar cost average into many stocks. These plans are called DRIP's (Dividend Re-Investment Plans). Many of the largest companies (Disney, IBM, Intel, Coke, etc.) allow you to buy shares directly from the company. Call them up and ask for a DRIP application. You can invest a fixed monthly amount here as well. If you were able to invest just $50 per month in the above four stocks, you would soon build up a large savings in these companies. Don't panic in times of trouble. There will be times when the stock market experiences severe corrections. You will be tempted to sell your positions at the absolute worst times. As the saying goes, "It is always darkest before the dawn." Do not try to time the market. Simply continue to invest the amount you allocated for dollar cost averaging. 250 years of precedence proves that patience will be rewarded.

5. **Asset Allocation**—How much should you put into bonds and how much should you put into stocks? A reliable rule of thumb is you take your age and subtract from 100 and that is the percentage you should put into the stock market. For example, if you are 30 you should have 70% in the index stock funds and 30% in a low cost bond fund.

6. **Portfolio Management**—After years of sticking to your plan of index fund investing and dollar cost averaging you will be able to build up a surprisingly large cash reserve. Avoid micro managing your investment positions. If you are truly thinking long term, short term moves in price should be meaningless to you. Stick to dollar cost averaging and concern yourself with other life pursuits. Your investments will take care of themselves over time.

7. **Stock Investments**—*Avoid high risk, get rich quick investments. It is not impossible but it is unrealistic to get rich quick.* By being disciplined and patient, you don't have to rely on luck to realize your dreams. Someday somebody will come to you and say I have inside information on a stock and you should put all your money into the investment. Billionaire investor Warren Buffett once said "If I had enough inside information I'd be broke in a year." Do not take big risks in stocks because there is a likelihood that they won't work out. If you lose half your capital on a foolhardy investment, it is very difficult to come back from that devastation. Furthermore, many people can't admit they made a mistake and hold onto their position as the stock goes lower and lower. Conversely, other people sell a stock position too quickly. Their stock drops 10% and they sell. The stock is then 50% up two years later. This is hard to keep straight. If you sell too early, you lose out. If you don't sell early enough, you lose out as well. Buy low, sell high. Buy high, sell higher. You can drive yourself crazy and lose a lot of money by investing in individual stocks. Many people, however, will reach a point where they will want to invest in stocks. While it is prudent to keep your most important assets (retirement, home savings, etc.) in index funds, there are

97

several general principles to follow if you do put a small portion of your cash into stocks.

8. **How Do I Pick Stocks**—*The key to investing in individual stocks is avoiding big losses. The key to avoiding big losses is to own many different stocks in several sectors. You must be diversified.* Even if one stock collapses you'll have 15 more to absorb the blow. If you don't have the capital to buy at least 15–20 stocks, stick with index fund investing. If you can buy at least 15 stocks, how do you figure out which ones to buy? There are many books which describe how to pick a stock. Before you run out and read them, be aware that there are also many books describing how to pick horses or how to win at blackjack. It's a gamble every time you pick an individual stock. The company you pick may run into problems (company risk) or the whole stock market may go through a down cycle (market risk). Let's use Microsoft as an example. This may have been the top company of the 90's. Lets say you are an investor ready to invest in the best stocks in the year 2000 and decide Microsoft is the biggest company in the best industry with the smallest risk. A couple months after your investment, all technology stocks (including Microsoft) suffer a major correction (market risk problem). You also discover that the government has recommended severe restrictions on Microsoft in a court case (company risk problem). You lose lots of money. Do you sell? Do you hold on to your position thinking that Microsoft will rebound? You may have a similar dilemma for just about any stock you choose. You must make sure that you don't put all your eggs in one basket. If you're diversified into the biggest companies in many sectors (drugs, technology, retail, oil, etc.) you have the best

98

chance of success. You mitigate both company risk and market risk.

9. **Saving for a Car, Home, College Fund, Etc.**—The above principles should provide you with the necessary strategy to invest so you can save up for most of life's major expenses. The key is to start saving early. For example, try to save a fixed amount every month long before Junior will begin college. Given the astronomical costs of college or buying a home, it is next to impossible to pay for these expenses without some type of loan. However, if you have invested and saved money over the years you reduce the amount of interest you'll pay on your loan. High interest payments paid out over many years can put you in a bigger financial hole than almost anything else. When you do have a mortgage or a college loan, try to pay off more than the minimum amount every month. For example, lets say you have a $100,000 thirty year mortgage to pay off. You pay approximately $1000 per month. If you increased this amount by even $50 monthly you can be done paying off your loan up to five years earlier. Check this out on the Internet. Many sites offer mortgage or loan calculators. You'll be amazed at the savings. The banks or car dealers won't tell you this because it means less interest payments for them.

You have the formula for wealth. It takes effort, good luck, solid investments, patience, perseverance and sacrifice. In the United States, virtually anyone who works hard and saves their money can become a millionaire over time. Is it worth trading a more balanced life for material success? Only you can answer that question. You must reach your own definition of prosperity.

CAREER

"Hi. I'm John Smith. I'm a plumber." Obituary: John Smith, 82, plumber, died yesterday in New York City. Society tends to define us by our occupation. The average person spends at least one-third of their life at work. It is virtually impossible to have a happy life if you have a miserable career. You can have a job you love or at least create some joy within your current job. You don't have to look forward to being 65 years old so you can retire and leave what you think of as your current prison. You don't have to thank God it's Friday. Follow the advice below and you will learn the secret of life known as **career**.

What Career Should You Pursue?

The answer to this question depends on your talents, goals and opportunities. You should also consider compensation levels and the future outlook of the business. The people who loved making buggy whips and ice boxes are out of a job. You don't need to be a visionary to see the future. You simply have to sit down and consider the current trends of industry. If you do this, you will be able to make a very good educated guess as to what careers will be profitable in the future.

101

For most people, a career choice based on compensation is a bad mistake. I'm sure you know a lot of wealthy people (lawyers, etc.) who hate their profession. A very important secret of life is to have a job that you enjoy. Most people enjoy a job that they perform well. Where are your talents? Everyone has received some gifts from above. Are you good with spatial relationships? Are you good with people? Are you good at Math or English? Write all your talents on a piece of paper. Then write jobs titles that match those talents. You can get a long list of professions right off the Internet to give you some ideas. Cross off the jobs that provide inadequate money to suit your needs and also those that have limited opportunity and a bleak business future. The jobs that remain are careers for you to consider.

WHITE COLLAR WORK

Job Search

The worst place to look for a job is in your local newspaper. Many advertised positions have already been filled. They are posted often for legal reasons. The odds are extremely long that you will find the start of a successful career in the employment section.

The best way to find great jobs is through connections. I'm sure you know the saying, "It's not what you know, it's who you know." What do you do if you have no connections in your chosen industry?

You must make your own connections. *Send letters to the heads of businesses in your chosen profession asking for an information interview.* Make it clear in your correspondence you are not asking them for a job. These interview requests are generally granted. When you meet with these corporate leaders, accumulate as much information as possible. What is good and bad about their business? What are the future prospects of the industry? After you receive the insider information, you may decide that this profession is not an avenue you would like to pursue. However, if you are still interested, ask them if they would have any suggestions as to how you could start a career in their business. If the interview goes well ask them for contacts. You will be able to gradually build a network in the industry. It won't be long until you have started an exciting new career.

A job search is full-time work. If you are unemployed, plan on working from nine to five Monday through Friday on this important effort. If you need money for expenses get a part-time evening job.

If you already employed in a job you want to leave, be prepared to use sick days to go on interviews. Use your office phone to contact potential leads. Don't make it obvious to your employer that you want to leave the job. Continue to work hard even if you hate your job. This is especially important if you plan to use you boss as a reference. These recommendations are often the final deciding factor for a new employer.

Send out hundreds of resumes and go to dozens of interviews. You must become immune to rejection. It's like sales. Every "no" means that you are that much closer to a "yes."

Interview

How can you improve your chances? The interview allows you to distinguish yourself from your competition. Preparation is very important. *Many recruiters decide in the first few minutes of the interview whether or not you will be considered.* The employer's goal is to find the best person to meet the company's needs. You must be prepared to be that individual. Try to be the solution to their business problem. Try to project yourself as the kind of person that would be the perfect fit for the available position.

You must "dress for success." The world is a shallow place and you are often judged by your appearance. Ignoring this fact will not help you get a great job. Don't try to be thrifty when choosing interview clothing. Make sure your suit is constructed of good material. You should dress with conservative colors. Men should wear gray, dark blue, or dark plaids. Do not wear a handkerchief in the breast pocket. Women should wear a conservative business suit or a dress below knee length. Choose a color that compliments your hair and skin tone (semi-gloss brown, tan, gray, or blue). Don't dress manly, but also don't dress like you are going out for an evening at the theater. Choose an outfit that makes you feel confident and comfortable within the above parameters.

Research the company extensively before your interview. Look up their Internet web site and read their annual report. The recruiter will be impressed by your knowledge of his/her company. As you answer questions, make sure you work this knowledge into the conversation. When the interview is completed, make sure you have prepared several questions to ask the recruiter. Make sure the questions concern the company. *You can always ask about salary, benefits, etc. after you are offered the job.*

Don't appear needy and desperate at the interview. This approach works no better in business than it does at dating. Try to promote the projection that you are a perfect fit for the job. You will work hard, but they are lucky to be able to hire you. Give the impression that you are in a position to choose among many opportunities, not desperate for the first available job. This attitude will help you not only to get hired, but also in your salary negotiations.

Salary Negotiations

Congratulations! You have received the job offer you have always wanted. No matter how much money they offer, ask for more. Negotiating salary is taken as a sign of maturity. You won't lose the opportunity by making an effort to receive more money. One secret of salary is, "Ask and you shall receive." You don't get many things without asking. Justify your request by detailing how your contributions are going to help the company. Remember there are other forms of compensation besides money. If you are unable to receive more money ask for more benefits or discounts on company products, etc. A lower salary with a great 401K is often more lucrative in the long run. *Your financial progress depends very much on where you start. If your lack of negotiation causes you to begin your career at a low salary it may take you years to receive the compensation that you are entitled.*

How to Do Well in Your Career

Now that you've secured a position in your chosen field with an adequate starting salary how do you proceed to have a successful, brilliant career? To have long term success you must find fulfillment at work. Work is not always pleasant. However, if you don't find your job rewarding you'll never be happy. Try to be creative with your job assignment. Invent ways of doing your work better and faster. Ask your boss for additional interesting responsibilities. Your initiative will be appreciated and rewarded. Not only will you be more fulfilled at work, you will be promoted at a more rapid rate.

Your success at work will be largely dependent on how you please your boss. Your boss is a human being (although sometimes you might not think so) and wants to look good to his or her boss. Do something each day to make your boss look good. Keep the boss informed on what you are doing at all times without becoming an aggravation. Try to solve problems before they reach your boss. If you have a problem that needs the attention of the boss, make sure that you offer possible solutions. Write a list of ideas on how the company can save money, be more efficient and increase sales. Present these ideas to your boss. He or she may take the credit for some of your brilliant ideas but it will benefit you down the road. No one likes a complainer. Always be positive and, if possible, never complain to your boss.

Manners in business are just as important as in personal life. Always be punctual for appointments. Return all phone calls within twenty-four hours. Answer letters within one week. Write thank-you notes frequently. When holding a meeting have all phone calls held. Explain in advance to your guests if there is a critical call you must interrupt the meeting to take. When making a speech don't go even one second over the scheduled time.

If you want a successful career learn to be a team player. If you make a mistake, NEVER refuse to take the blame. No matter how grievous your error, don't compound the situation by refusing to admit you're at fault. Apologize for this mistake and ask how it should be corrected. No matter how angry your associate is, apologizing and focusing on the solution usually defuses their wrath. If you blame the error on someone else they become infuriated and consider you a hopeless case who can't be taught and won't learn from your mistakes. Always encourage your colleagues and don't hesitate to congratulate them on a job well done. Praise the deed, not the person. Explain specifically what people have done to earn your appreciation. This will cause them to be excited by their work not just by your appreciation.

If you want to succeed in your career you must continue to develop your skills. Attend seminars, read the latest business best sellers and keep up with the trade journals. Stay abreast of the latest information affecting your industry. By constantly learning and developing you will not only do your job better but also enjoy it more.

Who do you actually work for? You work for your customers. They pay your salary. Always remember that when you are servicing a customer. Give them far more than they expect. Make your expectations for the treatment of customers clear to your entire staff. Put yourself in the customer's position. Solve problems before the customers complain, because many customers won't complain. They'll just stop being customers.

To succeed at work you must know how well you are doing. Insist on feedback from your boss. Don't wait for your annual review to obtain constructive criticism. When you receive criticism from your boss don't take it personally, but rather act to improve your performance.

If you follow the above advice you will no doubt have a long and productive career. Always remember that no one at the end of their life says, "I wish I had spent more time at the office." Though work is important, don't let it control you. Your family should always come first. You might say I work ninety hours a week for my family so they have a great future. You should be reconsider this position if you don't want to be divorced. Try to strive for a balanced life.

The secret of life regarding career is to make it a passion not an obsession. This will allow you to be successful personally, not just professionally.

BLUE COLLAR WORK

Blue collar work is a fabulous choice for a career. A skilled tradesman is always in demand. Plumbers, electricians, etc. command higher wages than most of their white collar peers. There is also great satisfaction when completing a job. You can see the results of your efforts on a more regular basis than white collar workers.

Unions

How do you become a professional tradesman? The easiest way is to join the union in the field of your choice (e.g. Plumbers and Steamfitters Local 127). You begin as an apprentice and learn the trade free of charge. Eventually you become a union member, licensed in your field.

A union provides great medical and pension benefits. These benefits are portable and aren't dependent upon any particular contractor. White collar work benefits vary from job to job and aren't portable.

Status

For some reason, blue collar workers enjoy lower status than white collar counterparts. You should not make career decisions based on uninformed public opinion.

Potential

Blue collar incomes are not capped by union wage contracts. Many plumbers, electricians and the like have become millionaires by opening their own businesses. A skilled tradesman creates incredible value. Work hard and develop your craft, and you will be limited only by the size of your ambition.

YOUR OWN BUSINESS

Many people wish they had their own business. They aren't happy with their employer (or boss) and believe they can do better, both financially and emotionally, on their own.

Financial Potential

If you own a successful business, you have a greater potential for a high income than you do as an employee. You are taking a greater risk (putting up capital, etc.), but if successful, you reap a greater reward.

Most businesses fail in the first year. You may not see a significant profit for 5–10 years. If you are patient, work very hard, have good luck and don't quit after the first sign of trouble you could make millions.

Emotional Factors

If you want your business to succeed, you must be willing to work VERY hard. Are you willing to devote this amount of time and energy to an endeavor? It may cause a strain on your family. The business may become the most important concern in your life. Entrepreneurship can be very rewarding but can also be challenging. Make sure you are prepared emotionally before undertaking such a commitment. If you are married, make sure your spouse is in total agreement with your decision to open a business.

Experience

It is certainly preferable to work in an industry for years before starting your own business. You can develop contacts and gain experience while on someone else's payroll. You can become an expert in your field before putting your own capital at risk.

Many businesses are not as glamorous as they appear to be to the outsider. Work experience in your chosen industry can prevent you from a life of misery.

Business Plan

A sound business plan is a critical element in any new company's success. You can hire a professional finance person to write a plan or do it yourself with the help of the Small Business Administration Internet web site.

The SBA suggests the body of the business plan can be divided into four distinct sections: 1) the description of the business, 2) the marketing plan, 3) the financial management plan, and 4) the management plan. Addenda to the business plan should include the executive summary, supporting documents and financial projections.

Perseverance

Patient effort is necessary once your business is established. It takes years for most businesses to realize their financial potential. You must be willing to fight through the early struggles and keep pressing forward. Once you achieve success, you must stay hungry and keep working diligently. If you get lazy, the competition may take away your customers.

TEN KEYS TO MINIMIZING STRESS AND ENJOYING YOUR JOB

1. Work efficiently so you don't have to take work home. Ending your day at 5:00 P.M. knowing you have two hours of paperwork to do at home is very deflating.

2. To work most efficiently, get into the office earlier than most so you can work in peace before the phone rings, etc. Nothing is more annoying than constant phone interruptions when you are trying to concentrate.

3. Always take lunch no matter how busy you are. Don't eat at work. An hour break is rejuvenating plus it's something to look forward to during a hard day. If practical, leave the office for lunch. Treat yourself to a nice meal now and then.

4. Do not kiss ass. You sacrifice your dignity and your boss will see right through this superficiality. Do your assignments with confidence and competence, and don't worry so much what others think of your work.

5. Never take a job for ego or money. School teachers are happier than lawyers and they work half the hours. If you take a job for $200,000 per year, expect to work for your salary.

6. Create job responsibilities you enjoy. Every job has some flexibility. If you like public speaking, volunteer to do presentations. Talk with your boss about how you can use your particular interests for the better of the company.

7. Do not take feedback about your performance personally. Be open to criticism. You are being given feedback about a task, not your skills.

8. Don't let irritating co-workers get to you. Remember you only have to work with them, not socialize with them. Don't try to be friendly with anyone you don't like. Stay away as much as you can.

9. Don't take a job as a stepping stone. You may have to climb a mountain for your desired promotion. Enjoy what you do now. Don't sacrifice ten years of enjoyment for the carrot at the end of the stick you may never get.

10. Make sure your number one goal is to have fun. Making money can be secondary. You can enjoy any job if you make having fun your number one priority.

CONVENIENCE

It's too bad there are only 24 hours in a day. With work, family and other life responsibilities, it's impossible to accomplish all we want each week. There is so much to do and so little time to do it. Is there a better way? Can you make your life a little easier? In order to do this, you need to know the **secrets of convenience**.

75 Ways to Simplify Your Life

Relationships

1. Don't put up with games in a relationship. You're presumably no longer in high school. There are other fish in the sea and the better ones don't play games. Adapting this strategy will save you a lot of time and heartache.

2. Don't confuse kindness for weakness in a partner. In the long run, nice people make better partners.

3. Stay away from affairs. If you want to complicate and ruin your life, be unfaithful to your partner. Fidelity equals simplicity and peace.

4. There is no room for jealousy in a relationship. Resentful suspicion is usually a sign of low self-esteem. If you are

jealous, you are alienating your partner. They may even try to make you jealous to establish control of the relationship. You can't control the actions of others. If you are jealous, keep it to yourself. Your lack of jealousy will be attractive to your partner. It gives them the impression that you are confident.

5. Learn to compromise. Meet the other person halfway.

6. Forgive yourself and others. Guilt and anger are burdens that you don't need to tote. Remember, we are all human.

7. Spend time with your children now so you won't have to visit them in jail later. The more time you spend with your child, the more likely he/she will grow up to be a good citizen. A child in trouble constantly complicates the parent's life. Take the time now to make sure that doesn't happen.

8. Give people plenty of notice. Try not to burden them with tasks at the last moment. They will complete what is expected of them if given enough time.

9. A relationship, like anything else, will die without maintenance. Never overlook the needs of your partner. Give them the proper love and attention now to avoid complications later.

10. Don't live your life to please others. You don't have to jump through hoops at people's commands. You'll never please everyone, so focus on pleasing yourself as long as you are doing what you know is right.

11. Mind your own business. Remember, curiosity killed the cat. Instead of worrying about everybody else's concerns, concentrate on your own. Don't engage in gossip. Wouldn't it be a simpler life if everyone minded their own business?

12. Don't get so busy with work and family that you forget your friends. If you are too occupied to do lunch, meet them for breakfast or happy hour instead. Nurture your friendships. Life can be a difficult trip and you will need them along the way.

13. Do not go on expensive dinner dates—except for special occasions. A fancy dinner will not make your date like you more.

14. If someone takes you out to dinner, accept the generosity of letting them pick up the tab. You can always treat the next time.

15. Don't expect to feel appreciated by other people, especially your spouse. Human beings take virtually everything for granted. Don't make this mistake. Appreciate yourself and others.

Finance

16. Don't take on a lot of debt. High monthly payments burden you with unneeded stress. Live modestly and you will make your life a lot more comfortable.

17. Try electronic banking to pay bills. You won't have to write checks every month. If you have a rent payment, you input the information once and the bank pays it every month without more work for you.

18. Hire someone to do your taxes. This will eliminate a lot of stress and aggravation. Tax laws change every year. The IRS makes it impossible for the lay person to keep up with the changes. A tax expert can find you legal deductions. These deductions may very well offset the cost of their services.

19. Don't buy a home as an investment. Purchase it because it is a comfortable place to live. If you buy a home, be prepared to work at least 3–5 hours a week on upkeep or to spend $3,000–$5,000 per year on maintenance. If you can't afford this expense, don't buy a home.

20. Don't buy a home just because you have the money. Rent until you are certain of your life situation. Buying severely restricts your freedom.

21. Don't worry about the stock market. Actively managing investments takes a lot of time and effort, and is of questionable value. Good investments take little time to manage.

22. Don't lend people money unless you are prepared never to be repaid. For some reason, people no longer feel an obligation to repay debts. If you make a loan, you are put in the inconvenient position of being a bill collector. If you want to lend money to someone in need, make it a gift.

23. Pay the extra couple of dollars for good food. If salmon that usually sells for $8.99 a pound is now $6.99 a pound, chances are its not fresh. Also, isn't it worth spending a little more on food if the result is much more delicious meals?

24. Don't open your own business if you want to simplify your life. Sometimes you can make more money with your own concern, but you always have more stress and complications. The government forms and regulations alone are enough to drive many businessmen insane. It is much simpler to find a job you like and draw a paycheck.

25. Don't be cheap. Spend moderate amounts of money to make life easier.

Self-Improvement

26. Model other people's successful behavior. Before attempting a project, ask for advice from knowledgeable sources.

27. Be flexible and roll with life's punches. Problems arise every day. Reacting emotionally will just ruin your mood and complicate matters.

28. Stop procrastinating. It's a lot harder to worry about doing something then just getting it done.

29. Schedule a worry time. Make sure it is well before you go to sleep. Don't complicate your life by worrying all day long. Unless you are delusional, you will have worries. If they arise outside your designated worry time, tell yourself you will put off being concerned until the next day.

30. Slow down and enjoy life. Most people are constantly concerned with the future or with thinking about the past. They do not concentrate on the moment. By focusing on the moment, you will feel more alive, happy and successful. Stop constantly looking at your watch, drive 5 miles per hour slower and do some relaxation exercises.

31. Never pass up an excuse to laugh. The average American laughs 15 times a day. Very happy people laugh over 200 times a day. You may think you need a Mercedes to be happy when all you really need is to laugh more. You must put yourself in a position to be exposed to humor. Read cartoons and joke books. Watch comedies on television. Try to see comedians in person. Tell people jokes and laugh at their humor. Don't take yourself too seriously.

32. Accentuate the positive. Try to associate with positive people. Your own negativity will grow unless you surround yourself with positive people. To keep a positive outlook, skip the nightly news. It is rife with depressing stories.

Use a newspaper to keep up on current events. Then you will be free to scan over the negative pieces and concentrate on the positive articles.

33. Don't be a liar. You need too good a memory. If you fabricate stories, it becomes hard to keep them all straight in your head. It is much simpler to tell the truth. Any abuse you suffer for the facts won't compare to the repercussions felt if caught in a lie later.

34. Stop being so concerned with what people are thinking about you. People are less concerned with you than you think.

35. Do less and enjoy your life more. Even Atlas couldn't carry the world on his shoulders forever. The more pressure you put upon yourself, the more complicated your life will be.

Health

36. If you desire thorough treatment from a doctor, bring them a gift. A box of candy will distinguish you from hundreds of patients. Doctors are human beings and will be influenced by your kind thoughts. If your consideration causes them to concentrate a little extra on your condition, it could save your life.

37. Have the doctor prescribe multiple refills for chronic medications. This eliminates the time and effort of many doctor's visits. Also, consider mail order pharmacies for your medication needs. Besides being less expensive, they are more convenient. You don't have to spend your day loitering around pharmacies waiting for your prescriptions to be filled.

38. Eat healthy now to avoid complications later. Why would you treat your body worse then you treat your car? Many

people use the finest products available for their car's engine but then poison their bloodstream with junk food. You can simplify your life in the long run by taking care of your body. Bad health is the biggest inconvenience of all. By taking care of yourself, you can gain ten or more years of good health. If you abuse your body, you will face physical and emotional pain at a much earlier age. Simplify your life by keeping yourself in good health. I know your salty and fatty snacks taste good, but are they worth a heart attack?

39. Prepare a written list of questions before you see your doctor. Most doctors try to rush you in and out of the office. Generally, this haste causes you to have some questions left unanswered. If you have a list, it is difficult for your doctor to neglect you. If all your questions are not answered, this complicates your life through increased worry and aggravation.

Organization

40. Try to be 15–20 minutes early for any appointment. This way, if you are running late you will not have to go into a mad, stressful rush. Your promptness will be appreciated by others.

41. Keep your desk clean. The more organized you are, the more efficient you will be. If something needs to be trashed, do so.

42. Keep instruction manuals in a file even after you have set-up an electronic device.

43. Put a copy of your address book on a computer disk. If you don't have a computer, still make a copy so if you lose your address book you won't lose all your important phone numbers.

44. Make a copy of everything that is in your wallet. If you ever lose your wallet or it is stolen, this will greatly simplify your life. You should copy all credit card numbers, driver's license, Social Security card and any documents in your wallet. You should also have the customer service numbers of your credit cards on file so that if they are lost or stolen you can report them missing immediately to limit your liability.

45. The Internet is a fabulous invention. Learn to use it effectively. You can research virtually any type of information on your computer.

46. Don't try to keep your entire schedule in your head. Purchase an appointment book.

47. Make a list before you go to the grocery store. Buy only what is on the list. This saves you time and money.

48. Do your mundane weekly tasks at the office. You want to protect your free time at home as much as possible.

49. Never hold a business meeting without an agenda. Without a written set of goals, a meeting usually turns into a bitching session. Once this occurs, nothing productive is accomplished.

50. Don't be a chronic "junk" saver. Learn to throw out useless items at home or office. It is much easier to locate something important if it is not buried under a mountain of junk.

51. Delegate assignments at work and home. Don't try to do everyone's job. Save your energy for the most important tasks.

52. Don't try to do too much at one time. Complete one job before attempting another. Hire someone to clean your house. You may hate cleaning. For the price of a movie and

a box of popcorn for two, you can hire someone to do your dirty work. The time you save on cleaning you can spend on more profitable endeavors.

Time Savers

53. See if you can work four 10 hour days instead of five 8 hour days. Many companies and government agencies offer this (flex) time. Can you imagine nothing but three day weekends?

54. If you are disabled or very busy, hire a neighborhood teenager to do errands for you. This will allow you to focus on more important efforts and not bankrupt you in the process.

55. Avoid reading junk mail. Sort through your mail near a trash can and deposit the unwanted letters into the appropriate receptacle. Just because someone sent you something, you are not obligated to read their correspondence.

56. It is easy to avoid being hassled by telemarketers. If someone calls and asks for Mr. or Mrs. X, simply tell them that they don't live here any more. If you are not sure it is a salesman, say you will take a message. You don't have to listen to anyone's pitch. You are not doing them a favor by hearing them out if you have no intention of buying.

57. When you approach a toll booth, head for the far right lane. Most people stay in their lane and go for the middle of the toll booth which results in a big delay. The far right side of the toll booth has normally only two or three cars ahead of you. If you stay in your lane and go through the middle of the toll booth, you may have to wait twice as long. After you pay your toll you will have plenty of time and distance to move left back onto the main highway.

58. Shorten your subscriptions. You may not have time to read all your magazines. You paid for them, so you may feel a burden to read them even if you are no longer enjoying the information. Don't review anything that you don't look forward to receiving in the mail.

59. Don't be a slave to the telephone. Use an answering machine or caller ID to screen your calls. Turn the ringer off on the phone if you want some peace and quiet. As a general rule, between 9:00 A.M. and 7:00 P.M., the chances are 50% that the call is a salesman, and 99% it is somebody asking you for something.

Travel

60. There are few things more valuable than a good car mechanic. Have your oil changed every 3,000 miles. A broken down car is one of life's most aggravating complications. Regular oil changes will go a long way toward preventing this from happening. Make sure you have an honest mechanic. Many businesses use inexpensive oil changes as an opportunity to promote unneeded car repairs. Find a mechanic you can trust and it will make your life much easier.

61. To avoid traffic and crowds, order pay-per-view movies rather than attending the live cinema. This approach also results in obvious financial savings.

62. Don't take optional car trips during rush hour. Obviously if you are commuting, these are not optional and cannot be helped. It is amazing, however, how many people run errands at 5:00 or 6:00 in the afternoon. Do your errands at off hours. Come home from the beach either very early or very late to avoid traffic. Always consider the time of day when making a trip. You will simplify your life by avoiding traffic jams.

63. Don't over pack for a trip. Just take the essentials. Buy mini-sized toiletries (shaving cream, toothpaste, etc.) for trips. You can always buy necessities on the road.

64. Don't be a typical man. Ask for directions.

65. Don't waste time looking for bargain vacations. Ads that offer cheap prices usually have hidden costs. Go to a trusted travel agent and pay a fair price for air and hotel. You should always be leery of "specials."

66. Try to get a hotel with a mini-refrigerator. You can keep breakfast and sandwich foods for a quick, cheap and safe meal.

67. Don't feel you need to see every sight so you have to run around each day and finish your vacation exhausted. Schedule a day of activity followed by a day of relaxation.

Fashion

68. Don't be a slave to fashion trends. Fashion is a business created to relieve women from their hard-earned money. If you don't enjoy following the fashion trends, just decide what looks good on you and stick with that approach. Don't let other people dictate your sense of style. Wear whatever makes you happy.

69. Try to have as many matching clothes as possible. It's very convenient to be able to grab a set of clothes in the morning without having to worry if it matches.

70. Make sure you decide on your wardrobe the night before. Make sure all of your clothes are available and presentable. You don't need to be put in a mad rush in the morning scurrying for your proper raiment.

71. If you are balding, don't try and hide your bald spot. A few strands of hair combed over your scalp looks foolish.

Short haircuts are the best solution.

Miscellaneous

72. Learn to enjoy your free time. Find a rewarding hobby. Don't just fill up your time with more tasks.

73. What is convenient for you is not always convenient for others. Don't cut corners at the expense of others.

74. If you plan on sleeping with someone, make sure you have protection. While this might seem "inconvenient" in the moment, an unplanned pregnancy will be somewhat more problematic.

75. Make a concentrated effort to take the aforementioned steps to make your life easier. Remember, a simple life is a happy life.

VITALITY

If you want to achieve vitality, you'll need to maintain a healthy lifestyle. The **secret of vitality** will give you all the ammunition you need to have a balanced diet, be at a healthy weight and adhere to an exercise program.

Nutrition

There are hundreds of different diets which claim to be the most healthy. Doctors seem to change their minds every year about the nutritional value of certain foods. Remember ten years ago when alcohol was considered unhealthy. Now one drink a day may prevent heart disease.

You can get caught up in counting calories, debating the nutritional value of foods and/or calculating the percentage of fat in your diet every day. This takes too much effort. We recommend simplicity when it comes to diet and nutrition. *What all healthy diets have in common is an emphasis on fruits and vegetables.* Dietary guidelines indicate 6–10 servings of fruit and vegetables daily. A serving can be as small as five strawberries, a tomato on a sandwich or a glass of orange juice. The reason that fruits and vegetables are so highly recommended is that they are packed with vitamins, minerals, antioxidants and fiber. They reduce your risk of heart disease, cancer and many other diseases. In addition, they help you maintain a healthy weight. How do you get more fruits and vegetables in your diet? Start with the first (and most important) meal of the day.

Breakfast

Breakfast is crucial because it revs up your metabolism so food is burned off more quickly the rest of the day. If you don't eat in the morning, your lunch is digested more slowly. You actually gain weight by skipping a light breakfast.

The easiest way to incorporate fruit into your breakfast is to put in on cereal. The best cereals are those which are all natural and high in fiber. Don't worry about the added vitamins and minerals which you see on many cereal labels. You should get all that from taking a daily multi-vitamin pill every morning.

Slice a banana and put some fresh berries on your cereal. Also, have a glass of orange juice (buy fresh squeezed if possible). It's 8:00 A.M. and you've already had three servings of fruit. If you don't have time for cereal, carry fruits you can eat on the run such as apples, bananas or peaches.

If you can, limit your caffeine in the morning. Caffeine does not give you enough of a physiological rush to give you that much more energy or to keep you more alert. If you must use caffeine, substitute tea for coffee. Tea has many more health benefits—especially green tea.

Lunch

Lunch is often the most unhealthy meal of the day since most people eat a take out lunch rather than preparing it themselves. Sandwiches seem to be the staple of most lunches. What you stuff between those two slices of bread can often make or break your diet. Ham, cheese and mayo on a roll is mostly fat and gives you almost no nutritional value. Turkey, lettuce, tomato and mustard is a lot better since it is lower in fat and incorporates two servings of vegetables.

We are not proposing that you only eat bland sandwiches for lunch very day. If you like roast beef, have it in moderation. When you do, just ask to have it with extra lettuce and tomato and light on the meat. It will taste exactly the same but it will be a healthier sandwich. Try to substitute a salad one day a week instead of a sandwich.

To get in your fruit and vegetables during lunch, bring a packet of vegetables from home. Baby carrots is one example of a vegetable that is easy to carry and store. However, you can just as easily bring raw broccoli, red peppers or string beans. We are not suggesting that you eat lunch like a rabbit. Just use the vegetables on the side with the rest of your meal. Also, don't skip lunch because you are too busy. Your hunger will catch up with you and you'll end up eating more at dinner.

Dinner

The less you eat out, the healthier your meals will be. By all means, enjoy going out to dinner. However, don't have take out food five nights a week. To make their food taste better and to add flavor, restaurants will often add butter, sugar, salt and fattening sauces to their dishes. Also, try not to eat dinner late at night because your metabolism has slowed and it is harder to burn off the calories. Try to have 8–10 glasses of water throughout the day.

Rather than suggest a menu (there are so many choices), we will just offer some guidelines. You must have Protein (lean meats, poultry, fish, dried beans, soy products), Carbohydrates (pasta, breads, grains, cereal, fruits, vegetables) and Fats (lean meats, olive oil, nuts) in your diet. The percentages of each vary depending on what you read, but it has become clear that you should limit your fat intake (20–25%).

Below are some foods that target the necessary nutritional needs. Try to incorporate these into your diet.

Vitamins & Minerals

Vitamin A—dairy products

Beta Carotene—carrots, sweet potatoes, spinach, cantaloupes

Vitamin C—citrus fruits, broccoli, tomatoes, melons, peppers

Vitamin D—low fat milk

Vitamin E—almonds, wheat germ, whole wheat bread, leafy green vegetables

Vitamin B6—poultry, fish, peas, dried beans

Vitamin B12—lean meat, fish, dairy

Calcium—low fat milk, broccoli, cauliflower, tofu

Iron—lean meat, poultry, fish, spinach

Heart Healthy Foods (may reduce your cholesterol level)

1. Fish like salmon, sardines, tuna, swordfish, etc.

2. High fiber foods like some cereals, oatmeal, dried beans, apples and most vegetables

3. One glass of wine a day. A substitute for this (if you don't drink) is grape juice

4. A couple cups of green tea

5. All fruits and vegetables (experiment until you find the ones you like best)

Weight Loss

You can lose weight without suffering. The secret is to eat all you want but of the correct foods. Foods are an acquired taste. You don't have to love fatty, sugary, salty substances. You can condition yourself to enjoy healthier foods. There is, however, an adjustment period of a couple of weeks. At first, you'll find you crave fatty foods as your system adjusts to decreased fat. After a couple of weeks, you won't have that same desire and won't feel as hungry.

Cutting fat from your diet will lower your risk of cancer, may prevent a heart attack and will definitely help you to maintain a healthier weight. The FDA has mandated that stores label all packaged foods with nutritional information. Included in this data is the fat content. Most Americans receive more than 40% of their calories from fat. This is the main reason for the high rate of heart disease and obesity in the United States.

You should try to obtain no more than 20% of your calories through fat. In days gone by, this would have meant great sacrifice. Low fat meals resembled sawdust. This has changed for the better as companies have learned to make delicious low fat food. Examine the frozen food section at your local supermarket and you'll be pleasantly surprised. Many delicious frozen dinners are low fat.

When you want fresh food, focus on fruits, vegetables, fish and poultry. If you don't want to cook, many specialty markets have tasty meals that are made with these ingredients. Try to stay away from fried foods. When you eat red meat, get the leanest cut available. If you fry at home, use nonfat cooking oil.

Try to stay away from unnecessary sugars like soda, candy and high calorie desserts. Satisfy your sweet tooth with the natural sugars in fresh fruit. If you want a piece of candy substitute sugar free gum.

There are four steps to accomplishing permanent weight loss.

1. You must achieve a thorough understanding of the role metabolism plays in weight control.
2. You must prepare yourself psychologically for permanent weight reduction.
3. You must learn the proper foods to eat for permanent weight loss.
4. You should begin an exercise program to raise your metabolism for weight control.

Role of Metabolism

Why do some people eat very little and still remain heavy? Why do others eat all the time and still remain thin? Why do people tend to put on weight as they get older? Why did your uncle lose twenty-five pounds when he quit drinking beer? The answer to all of these questions is **metabolism.**

Metabolism is the rate you burn off food when you are at rest. Some people have a faster metabolism than others, so they can eat more and maintain a good weight. Metabolism slows with age, so it's natural to gain weight as you get older.

Alcohol (even in small amounts) also slows your metabolism. Even two beers a day will have a negative effect on your weight. Although implied otherwise in advertisements light beer is no less fattening than regular beer. Light beer has less calories but slows the metabolism just as severely. Two or three drinks a day may not harm your health but will definitely cause you to gain weight. If losing weight is really important to you, you should consider discontinuing drinking. If you enjoy drinking too much to quit, you should consider cutting back to once or twice a week.

Mentally Preparing for Weight Loss

Diets are almost never successful. Being thin isn't worth being hungry. No one can enjoy life and exist in a mode of self-sacrifice indefinitely. People lose weight then put it back on. They live with an all or nothing mentality. Either they are dieting or not dieting. To be successful with long term weight loss you must undergo a lifestyle change.

Set reasonable goals for yourself. Honestly evaluate your metabolism and genetic predisposition. Don't compare yourself to women or men in magazines. Their gaunt appearance is mostly due to camera angles, drugs, genetics, and operations. If you set an unrealistic goal for yourself you can become frustrated and return to your previous unhealthy lifestyle.

Take a good look at your eating habits. Do you eat out of boredom? Do you eat when you are depressed to elevate your

131

mood? Do you eat when you're angry? You might have answered yes to all of these questions. Substitute other methods for controlling anger, depression or boredom. Exercise is an excellent replacement for you to use at these times. Do you hate exercising? Read a book or go shopping. If you want to lose weight, you must not eat for any other reason besides hunger.

When you are hungry do you eat until you become full? You should eat only until you are no longer hungry, not until you become full. By doing this you will not only control your weight, you will also improve your overall health. Eating small frequent meals greatly lessens the burden on your internal digestive organs. Light, healthy snacks during the day also minimizes hunger.

The only time it is worthwhile going hungry is at night. Try to break the habit of late night snacks. Your metabolism slows at night and a late night snack results in weight gain. If you are extremely hungry don't torture yourself. Eat something light. If possible, abstain from eating at night. If you are filled with desire say to yourself, "go to bed hungry—wake up lighter."

Many people equate staying in shape with dieting. While healthy eating is an important component of fitness, dieting is not the only answer. In fact, it may not be healthy at all if you don't do it properly. Staying slim is not always equal to being healthy. Everyone who is serious about fitness should try to incorporate some kind of exercise program into their routine in addition to watching their diets. Exercise will not only burn calories but also, as stated earlier, improve your metabolism.

The Importance of Exercise

The **secrets of vitality** do not lie solely with good eating habits. Regular exercise is crucial as well. *The benefits of healthy eating and regular exercise combined is infinitely greater than either of them alone.* While maintaining a healthy lifestyle is not easy, the benefits are worth it. You will look better, feel more confident and have more energy.

It is not fun to be wheezing when walking up a flight of stairs, to be embarrassed about wearing a bathing suit, and to listen to your doctor lecture you year after year about the risks of heart disease. The basic idea of being fit is to improve the quality of life. You may also improve your chances of living longer but this is certainly no guarantee.

While most people understand the benefits of regular exercise, very few people work out consistently. Some of the most common reasons people don't work out regularly are:

1. I'm too tired
2. I don't have the time
3. I've tried before and it doesn't work
4. I have a bad knee, back, etc.
5. It's too much effort
6. It's not fun
7. I'm too old
8. I'm too out of shape
9. I can't stick to it
10. A gym costs too much
11. There's no place to work out where I live

The secrets of fitness will help you to combat all of the above excuses. You will feel more motivated and be able to take some action to improve your level of fitness.

First of all, what you should be happy to know is that the types of lengthy exercise programs recommended in most books and fitness magazines are unnecessary for being healthy. Granted, they will bring you a higher level of fitness but there is little correlation between longer work outs and great health. You can be very healthy without training like an Olympic athlete.

Recent studies have consistently shown that 15–30 minutes of jogging (even if you alternate with walking) brings you almost as many health benefits as running 5 miles. Twenty minute workouts on the nautilus equipment will improve your muscle size, tone, and improve metabolism.

The bottom line is that maintaining fitness is not that hard. It is not as easy as the infomercials seem to suggest when they show a model bending a rubber tube and explaining that five minutes a day with the "Wonder Tube" (which costs you $79.95) will create the body you desire. Never buy any fitness equipment advertised on TV. They are a waste of time and money.

The easiest way to achieve fitness is to lead an active lifestyle. It is not even that important what type of workout you choose. Some people enjoy brisk walks or hiking. Others swear by the gym. Many people love the solitude of a peaceful run, bike ride or swim. The more competitive types enjoy a game of basketball or tennis. *Whatever you do, you will reap the rewards as long as you sufficiently increase your heart rate.* Unfortunately, this means that playing first base on your company softball team and going out for beers after the games doesn't count. Neither does walking around the malls shopping for a couple of hours and stopping for bon-bons along the way.

Basically, we are recommending a very simple routine for people whose goal is to improve or maintain their level of fitness. Do any workout that increases your heart rate sufficiently 2–3x per week for your aerobic benefits. In addition, do some kind of weight training 2x per week to increase muscle tone and improve metabolism. *All it takes is a half hour 3–4 times a week and you can improve and/or maintain a healthy level of fitness.*

Those of you with more generous proportions may have read the last section and said to yourself that there is no way these short workouts will transform my body so it's not even worth trying. Your dead wrong. It may take longer, but the method can work for anyone.

The worst thing you can do if you are out of shape is give up hope and do nothing. Time passes and you grow more out of shape. You fail on worthless liquid diets where all you get to eat is a foul tasting, 50 calorie chocolate milkshake. You keep telling yourself that one day you'll get in shape. That day never comes and you've gone through many years of feeling sluggish, tired, unhealthy and guilty whenever you eat a piece of cake.

If you are able to maintain a consistent workout schedule and eat reasonably healthy, you'll see the pounds melt away over time. The problem with most people is that they expect immediate results. They get on the scale after a week of working out and eating right and they've gained two pounds. Half the people quit right away. Those that continue get very frustrated because it's taking too long. They think that if they can put on twenty pounds in a month they should be able to lose twenty pounds in a month.

The secret to maintaining your fitness routine is to set a realistic long term goal (to run a 5K race or even to be able to play a round of golf). This creates purpose, but not always enough motivation. To motivate yourself, short term goals are the key (to run for 10 minutes without stopping, to be able to do 30 pushups). Write your progress down. Compare your first week to your fourth week. Work out with a partner if possible.

The important thing is to use as many tricks as possible to avoid quitting. Beyond setting goals, monitoring your progress and working out with a friend, there are several other techniques that will help you to avoid "burn-out."

1. Check with your doctor to assess the risks of your proposed exercise program. Injuries are one of the biggest setbacks to getting in shape.

2. Try to build a base. If you have not exercised in five years, don't try to run three miles in twenty minutes. You'll only end up sore and disappointed. For example, if you choose running, try alternating running with walking. Make sure you start out light and moderately increase your workouts.

3. Vary your exercise program. If you get bored with one form of exercise, try another. Replace running with hiking or swimming. One of the biggest pitfalls of most exercise routines is they get boring after a while. Switching your routine can re-invigorate you.

4. Don't look at the scale for the first month of your program. It is common to actually gain a little weight during the first couple of weeks after starting to exercise since you are turning fat into muscle and may be eating a little more (albeit healthier) food for energy.

5. Do your workouts at the same time each week. Make it a part of your regular schedule so you are less likely to blow it off. Schedule a half hour for yourself every other day and keep it consistent. Make it a priority.

6. Don't give up even though the benefits may be occurring slowly. Remember that the internal benefits (heart, lungs, etc.) which you may not see are the crucial pieces to health. Weight is certainly a part of this, but improvements in this area may take some time. Even though it only took three months to put it on, it's going to take longer to take it off.

Great health is achieved through healthy eating habits and a consistent fitness routine. The combination of both will allow you to live a life full of **vitality**.

LONGEVITY

Once you've completed the *Secrets of Life* you'll need some time to implement the lessons you've learned. The longer you live the more time you'll have to benefit from your knowledge. This chapter will teach you the **secrets of longevity**.

Unfortunately, the most important key to longevity is beyond your control. Genetics play an integral part in life expectancy. How long did your parents and grandparents live? Most likely you'll reach a similar age range.

You can improve your chance at longevity by taking care of yourself. Don't smoke cigarettes. They are proven killers. They are the only product that's lethal if used exactly how it's directed. Limit your consumption of alcohol. More than a couple of ounces a day poses a serious health risk. Don't take street drugs. Get plenty of rest. Watch what you eat. Think about what you are doing to your system before you shove that next triple cheeseburger into your mouth.

Don't take foolish chances. Many people say, "I'll eat anything I want because I'm going to enjoy life and you can't live forever." Many of the same people are dead at fifty of a heart attack. You can avoid much reckless behavior by not acting on impulse. Consider what you are doing at all times and you are more likely to make healthful decisions.

Make sure you receive regular and thorough medical treatment. Align yourself with a doctor you trust early in life. Don't try to diagnose yourself, and if you are feeling poorly see the doctor right away. *Even if you are not ill, make sure you get an annual physical exam. By the time symptoms surface it is too late to treat many illnesses.* Don't be like an ostrich sticking its head in the sand. Find out if you have medical problems and start early intervention. This could make a difference between an early call and a long life.

ENEMIES OF LONGEVITY

Coronary Artery Disease

The most common kind of heart disease is coronary atherosclerosis. It is the leading cause of death in the western world. The disease is not necessarily part of the aging process. It affects more men than women. It occurs more often in whites, the middle aged or elderly. Coronary atherosclerosis occurs most frequently in affluent populations with diets high in total fat, saturated fat, calories, cholesterol and refined carbohydrates. The risk of death from coronary artery disease is two to six times greater among smokers than nonsmokers and appears to be proportional to the number of cigarettes smoked per day. Hypertension is also a prime risk factor for the disease. Cigarette smoking combined with hypertension increases your risk by a factor of fourteen times.

While no single cause of atherosclerosis has been found, the development of the disease is closely linked with cholesterol levels. There are two types of cholesterol: LDL or "bad cholesterol" and HDL or "good cholesterol." LDL (low density lipoproteins) causes blockage of arteries while HDL (high density lipoproteins) cleans out the arteries. The lower your LDL levels and the higher your HDL, the better your chances of avoiding atherosclerosis. Your doctor can tell you the steps you can take to improve your cholesterol levels.

There are many treatments available for victims of coronary artery disease. They include drug therapy and surgical intervention. Even with proper and aggressive medical treatment, coronary artery disease often progresses to heart attack and/or heart failure. *Prevention is the key. Don't smoke, control high blood pressure, and reduce elevated cholesterol and triglyceride levels. Exercise moderately to help with weight control and circulation.*

Coronary artery disease begins to develop as early as in the third decade of life, particularly for people with family histories. Is the small pleasure of your gluttonous diet worth putting yourself in grave danger? Condition your mind that eating right is more pleasurable than eating unhealthy, deadly foods. Why would you treat your own body worse than you would treat your car? You regularly service your car to protect the engine. Shouldn't you protect your own heart as well?

You may be sitting there thinking, "I can't give up the salty, fatty foods I love so much." Healthy or unhealthy foods are an acquired taste. You may be in the habit of eating poorly. Healthy foods taste bland to you. Eating healthy for one month will change your thinking for life. Not only will the healthy food begin to taste better and better, your old dietary habits will begin to repulse you.

Try an experiment that may save your life. Eat healthy for one month and if you are not happy with the result, go back to your own dangerous way of life. It's our belief that once you try this way of living you will look better, feel better and drastically reduce your chance of heart disease.

Cancer

Cancer is second to heart disease as a cause of mortality and is a leading cause of death in young children. The most common sites for the development of malignant tumors are the lung, breast, colon, uterus, oral cavity and bone marrow. The basic origin of cancer is undetermined but many potential causes are recognized. More than 80% of cancer cases are attributed to cigarette smoking (lung cancer), exposure to carcinogenic chemicals, ionizing radiation and ultraviolet rays from the sun (skin cancer). There is also a genetic predisposition in families for the disease.

Listed below are several warning signals that may indicate cancer.

1. Change in bowel or bladder habits
2. Unusual bleeding or discharge
3. Obvious changes in a wart or mole
4. Thickening or a lump in a breast or elsewhere
5. Prolonged nagging cough or hoarseness
6. A sore that does not heal
7. Difficulty in swallowing or indigestion

Obviously these signals can be attributed to other causes besides cancer so don't panic if you have a sore throat with a nagging cough. However, if you do suffer from any of these symptoms see a doctor right away.

If you are ever diagnosed with any type of cancer, look into all the possible treatment options. Don't blindly take the advice of a doctor. Often, doctors have a stake in the type of treatment they recommend. If they were trained in a certain procedure, they will probably advocate for it. Always get a second opinion and gather all the information you can about your condition. The Internet has become an excellent source of medical information.

Early intervention is critical when dealing with cancer. Many forms of cancer can be cured if found before they metastasize. If you have cancer, it won't disappear on its own. Don't ignore the warning signals. Seek treatment right away and you can become one of the millions of cancer survivors.

Stroke

A stroke is caused by a blockage of the blood vessels leading to the brain. There are four warning signals of stroke:

1. temporary loss of speech (trouble in speaking or understanding speech)
2. temporary loss of vision particularly in one eye
3. unexplained dizziness, unsteadiness or sudden falls
4. temporary weakness or numbness of the face, arm and leg on one side of the body

Many fatal strokes are preceded by little strokes which have warning signals that are experienced days, weeks or months before the more severe event. Prompt medical or surgical attention to these symptoms may prevent a fatal or disabling stroke. If you have any of the above warning signals see a doctor right away. There are risk factors that can be changed concerning a stroke. The control of high blood pressure will greatly reduce the risk of a stroke. Good management of heart disease and diabetes reduces the risk of a stroke.

There are some risk factors that cannot be changed. The risk of stroke is greater in men than in women. The risk of death and disability from a stroke is much greater among Afro-Americans than among white Americans. If you are in a high risk group take special precautions to eliminate the risk factors that you can control. High blood pressure causes heart attacks, heart failure, and stroke. Have your blood pressure tested regularly. There are medications that can control blood pressure very effectively.

AIDS

HIV, the virus that causes AIDS, can easily be avoided. You must avoid sexual contact or sharing needles with someone infected with the virus. HIV is not spread through casual contact. You can live with a person, eat with them and/or hug them with no chance of catching the disease.

The safest way to avoid HIV is to be sexually abstinent. Abstain from sex until you are in a relationship. Then both partners can be tested for HIV and if negative can safely have sex with one caveat. Once infected it can take up to six months to convert to HIV+ status. A test in the interim could be a false negative.

It is probably unrealistic to expect most people to abstain from sex. Condoms are therefore the uniform of the day. Young people should be educated about protected sex at an early age. Condoms, if used correctly, are virtually 100% protective against the AIDS virus.

The world has made incredible progress in the treatment of HIV in record time. HIV is no longer a death sentence. Confirm your HIV status and, if positive, receive treatment. Protease inhibitors often bring blood levels of HIV virus down to undetectable amounts. Current available treatment must be continued for life and it has not yet been confirmed whether it will be successful long term.

Accidents

Most accident fatalities are automobile related. Does that mean you should not drive your car? Of course not. You should simply take some precautions.

1. Avoid driving drunk.
2. Don't drive angry or tired.
3. Don't speed or drive in a reckless fashion.
4. Don't drive through red lights.

Many automobile accidents are unavoidable. Sometimes you are simply in the wrong place at the wrong time. However if you follow the above advice you will drastically reduce your chances of being the victim of an accident.

Murder

It's a rough world. Murders take place every day. Many murders are caused by rage and jealousy. You should be able to avoid being one of these victims by taking some simple precautions:

1. Don't stay in abusive domestic relationships. Violence begets violence. Leave before the beatings turn into murder.

THE SECRETS OF LIFE

2. Don't sleep with other people's spouses. Jealousy is a powerful emotion and can drive many normal people into criminal acts.

3. Avoid activity in illegal businesses such as the drug trade. Most murders are drug related. Stay out of the narcotics world.

4. If possible stay out of bad neighborhoods, especially at night. Try to avoid being in the wrong place at the wrong time.

5. Don't wear flashy jewelry and watches. Vanity and ego encourages us to display what we've accumulated materially in life. Do this at your own risk. Many unfortunates won't be happy for your success but will instead decide to steal your expensive items. If desperate enough, they will murder you to do such.

Suicide

Many suicides are committed by the old and sick. These people decide that their painful infirmities make it too difficult to continue living. For these people, there is no hope of recovery or improvement. They have nothing in this world to look forward to except increasing physical discomfort.

Many physically healthy people also commit suicide. They share the same feelings of hopelessness and helplessness as the older terminal victims. If you find yourself considering suicide seek help immediately. You may have a very treatable form of depression. Watch for early signs of suicidal intent. They include: depression, expressions of guilt, tension, agitation, poor sleep habits, loss of appetite, loss of energy and direct or indirect threats to commit suicide.

146

While life may be unbearable for the time being for a person contemplating suicide, there may be a light at the end of the tunnel. Try therapy. Take medications if recommended. Give yourself time to improve. Seek support of friends and family.

TEN KEYS TO A LONG, HEALTHY LIFE

1. Have good genes.

2. Don't smoke and don't have more than two alcoholic drinks per day.

3. Eat a balanced diet low in saturated fats.

4. Exercise to improve aerobic conditioning.

5. Get adequate sleep. Lack of rest weakens your immune system, making you susceptible to serious illness. Also, the body heals itself from muscle and tissue damage during sleep.

6. Have your blood pressure checked regularly after age 30. If your blood pressure is elevated, take proper medication.

7. Don't take foolish risks such as driving drunk, doing recreational drugs, extra marital affairs, sex without condoms, etc.

8. Don't assume your body is infallible. Many symptoms are undetectable until it's too late. Many diseases are treatable if caught early enough. Prevention is the key and is achievable through the proper lifestyle.

9. Make sure you have good medical care. Don't skimp on any exams, no matter how routine, just to save a few bucks. Even a small mole which you have had for years could be skin cancer. Better safe than sorry. If you can't afford insurance, find a way to get on Medicaid or Medicare.

Try to see a doctor who you are comfortable with. Don't just go to any quack because they are on your HMO.

10. When you're a senior citizen, ask for assistance if you need help climbing a flight of stairs or shoveling snow. Swallow your pride. There is no shame in being aged. If younger people rush you to do things faster, hit them with your cane.

You have learned many secrets of longevity in this chapter. If you follow the above advice there is a great chance you will live a longer life. However, no one stays in this world forever. It would benefit you greatly to develop a philosophy about death and dying. Most people are afraid of death because of a fear of a lack of a future and the unknown. Condition yourself through prayer and spiritual study that there is an afterlife. When you accomplish this goal you will have developed the most rewarding philosophy of your life.

While you're in this world, live life to its fullest. Follow the advice of this chapter but don't be so worried about death that you forget to live. Let God be in charge of your death and you be in charge of your life. When HE wants to meet you personally, HE'LL make the call. Seize all the happiness you can from this life and take comfort from the fact that when you do move into eternity there is endless joy waiting for you.

ADVERSITY

I t's easy to be happy and productive when everything is going well. Unfortunately, there will be times of hardship as well. One of the most crucial secrets of life is to be able to handle adversity. To a large extent, how you are able to deal with misfortune will define you as a person. Adversity can be separated into trials, tribulations, and tragedies.

Trials can be considered the normal problems of everyday life. They are the little aggravations that seem to burden us all. Everyone has problems. The only people without them are in the cemetery. Your goal should not be to eliminate all your problems because it is impossible. Life is a series of challenges from cradle to grave. In many ways this is what makes life so interesting. As you progress through life, every problem you solve will be replaced by a new and generally more interesting one. So don't be frustrated by your problems. Look at them as puzzles and challenges. Every problem is an opportunity for success. When you solve a problem enjoy the feeling of accomplishment.

A problem is a situation that presents difficulty, uncertainty, or perplexity. The uncertainty provides a great opportunity. Next time you have a particularly perplexing problem relax and try to get into a creative state of mind. Relaxation is important because excessive anxiety curtails creative thinking and problem solving. Write down your problem on a piece of paper. For five minutes write down every possible solution that comes to mind however far-fetched. These solutions should solve not only your current problem but also offer insight into other challenges. A scientist for 3M invented a glue that only worked temporarily. This "failure" became the billion dollar product Post-It Notes. Pfizer's drug Viagra is one of the top pharmaceuticals in the United States. It's discovery was accidental. They were testing the drug for another purpose and found it increased blood flow to the penis. Problems force you to think creatively. You can move mountains by being in this creative state of mind. Problems cause you to grow as a person. Embrace them, don't be afraid of them.

Tribulations (life's most critical issues) and **Tragedies** (adversity so egregious that full recovery is impossible for most people) cannot be solved through rational problem solving. You'll need time for emotional healing, patience and support of loved ones. For some tragedies, there are no secrets. There are only ways of easing the pain. For others, there are some proven methods to help you overcome the problem.

Adversity is an unavoidable part of life. In everyone's life, some rain must fall. When it does, do you try to find an umbrella or just stand there wet and feeling sorry for yourself. In other words, how do you cope with the adversity that you will inevitably face?

How many alcoholics, drug abusers and smokers know they should quit but never do? How many people turn financial loss into an even bigger crisis by destroying their relationships as well? How many terminally ill people curse there fate and waste the time they have left?

A common trait in all people who can best cope with adversity is resiliency. Resiliency is the ability to bounce back from any setback. It is being able to mobilize all your emotional resources and tackle your problems head on. What does it take to become resilient in times of dire stress?

First of all, it takes an attitude that you can deal with any challenge that is presented. It is having confidence and faith in the resiliency of human nature. A resilient person can see the sun through the clouds. He/she can think about a situation in the most optimistic way possible. Christopher Reeves has participated in numerous charitable causes after he became disabled. He has no use of his arms and legs so he makes use of his brain and his heart. Did Stevie Wonder give up because he was blind? He cannot not see but he can sure sing.

How do you create positive thinking in times of adversity? It is a matter of perception. You will, no doubt, have to go through periods of depression, anger and/or anxiety when dealing with a life tribulation or tragedy. That is part of being human. We all feel sad if we suffer a loss. We all get angry if we believe life has treated us unfairly. We all have doubts that we will be able to get through the emotional pains of a tragedy.

The trick is not to allow these feelings to consume you. This is not easy. It takes training your mind to think in a different way. For example, former quarterback Boomer Esiason's young son has Cystic Fibrosis (a debilitating life threatening illness). Boomer decided to champion finding a cure. He has raised awareness and millions of dollars in donations to help research the disease. He can say to himself that there is nothing he can do to make his son healthy, but there is a lot he can do to make his son's life happy. In addition, he has spun this tragic personal situation in a way to help other families who are suffering.

151

Dealing with this tragedy could have destroyed the Esiason family. Instead, they decided to make it an enriching, rewarding and challenging journey.

For any type of adversity, it is much more empowering to think how to make the best of a situation than to lament about why the disaster happened to you. For example, lets say you suffer from financial ruin. Don't focus on what you've lost. Instead, concentrate on what you still have. If you had the ingenuity to make all the money in the first place, you have what it takes to get back on your feet. A resilient person may decide that this is an opportunity to make a new life. The slate is wiped clean and now he/she can go in another direction that may prove to be as fulfilling as making all the cash.

When you are suffering from adversity, you may say that is impossible to think positively. This is self-defeating and will only keep you mired in your misery longer. Begin to think about the situation differently. Train your mind to ask different questions. Don't ask, "Why did this happen to me?" Ask instead, "What personal strengths can I use to climb out of this hole?"

When you are training your mind to ask these empowering types of questions, try to make them action oriented. Ask yourself "what can I do" instead of asking yourself "how long will it be before I feel better." Taking action creates confidence that you can to do something to help yourself and/or those in need of your help.

It is only advisable to take action, however, when you are able to ask positive, empowering questions. If you are in a bad frame of mind, taking action may only make things worse. For example, lets say your spouse died in a car accident. You suffer extreme pain of loss. You go through a long mourning period that seems never ending. You may ask yourself, "How can I stop feeling so bad?" Your answer will depend on your mind set. You may say, "Daily inebriation will help me to forget my pain." However, if you are thinking in an empowering way you may say to yourself, "Even though I'm still feeling my wife's loss, I must still go on with my life." Even though you are devastated, you find your own personal way to cope with the tragedy in a positive way.

After you have trained your mind to perceive adversity in a more empowering way, you must use your resources to help you out of the abyss. There is a saying from the movie "Wall Street" that goes, "Man looks into the abyss and sees nothing staring back at him. That's when man finds his character and that's what keeps him out of the abyss." This means that you have two choices when hit with adversity. Get the best of it or let it get the best of you. If you have developed character, you will have the ability to work through your problem.

One of the best resources for help is other people. It could be a family member, a trusted friend, a clergyman, another sufferer of a similar tragedy or a therapist. Support from people gives you strength. It helps you to feel less alone. These compatriots may also be able to give you valuable advice, especially when you are in a state where you are not thinking clearly. Furthermore, if you have joined a support group that focuses on your particular tribulation or tragedy, you will meet people who have successfully worked through the problem. Don't try to reinvent the wheel yourself. What worked for others in your support group will also work for you. Model their behavior and you will be able to overcome the adversity.

Let's say you have been able to think about your situation in a better way, you are asking empowering questions, you are taking positive actions toward resolution and you are seeking the support of others. You still can't get over your divorce, recover from your depression or consistently stay on the wagon with drinking. What now? Don't be impatient. Solutions to adversity takes time. If you could resolve your adversity in a couple of days then it wouldn't be adversity. Take comfort that you are on the right track. Don't beat yourself up if you have a bad couple of days coping with your problem. Most importantly, don't give up. The only way you can be sure that your adversity will be unending is to quit.

To help get you started, the following sections will offer a brief description of many of the tribulations and tragedies that people may face in their lives. Keep in mind that is impossible and insulting for us to offer specific **secrets** for dealing with a disease like cancer or a problem as debilitating as drug addiction. We are not attempting to address the following conditions in enough breadth or depth so that you will find an immediate solution from reading these pages. It is imperative that you consult a specialist in your particular area of strife.

We do hope, however, to point you in the right direction. So if you are faced with an IRS audit, chronic physical pain, domestic abuse or any other tribulation or tragedy in life read on. Your mastery of these lessons will guide you through the darkest points in your life.

IRS Audits

Fifty percent of the people polled responded that they'd rather be mugged than audited by the IRS. This position is based on ignorance. With the right information, you can easily survive an audit. First, don't cheat on your taxes. The interest and penalties are too severe if caught. That doesn't mean that you shouldn't take every possible deduction available by law. It is worth the investment to hire a competent tax advisor. He or she should be able to alert you to every deduction. Don't try to do it yourself because the laws change virtually every year.

If you are audited send your tax advisor as your representative. This will prevent the auditor from going on fishing expeditions. Your advisor will bring all documentation necessary to prove the point being audited. If you are in attendance the auditor may ask you probing questions on other tax matters. Acting as your representative, your tax advisor can simply state he/she has no other knowledge than that of the issue being audited.

At some point of the audit your advisor should make it clear that he/she is familiar with the appeals process. You can appeal the auditor's decision to the IRS Appeals Division. Then you can appeal their ruling by petitioning the tax court. Each of these filings gives you a chance to negotiate a lower settlement of your tax bill. The average appeal results in a 40% reduction in taxes. Only 8% of taxpayers appeal because they are unaware of the process. Auditors are evaluated by how many cases they close with the taxpayer. The auditor will usually give you a more sympathetic hearing to avoid an appeal.

Pain

Everyone will face a bout of critical pain in their lifetime. Headaches, backaches, arthritis and others are among the most common infirmities suffered today. Most people's pain is transitory and relieved by rest and over-the-counter medication. However, there are millions of people in the United States that suffer from chronic pain. Chronic pain can cripple you and ruin your life. It is one of the leading causes of suicide. Fortunately there are methods to improve your situation.

Pain is a symptom of damage in the body. Don't just self-medicate with large amounts of aspirin or Tylenol and hope it goes away. Besides often being ineffective, these OTC remedies can have terrible side effects over time. Large amounts of Tylenol over years can destroy your liver. Large amounts of aspirin over years can destroy your kidneys.

Make sure you see a doctor to get an accurate diagnosis of the cause of your pain. This is often more difficult than it sounds. You may need to see a neurologist or orthopedist. If someone recommends surgery get a second opinion. Don't go to another surgeon for another opinion. They are often prejudiced in favor of the knife. A neurologist can generally offer you accurate answers. They can tell you the chance of a successful operation. Some procedures like carpal tunnel surgery are almost universally successful. Other operations such as difficult back problems and nerve damage are often unsuccessful. You should be aware of all the facts. What is the chance this operation will fix the underlying cause and remove your pain? What are the risks? What is the chance this procedure will lead to more operations down the road? Unfortunately many people will have chronic pain for a lifetime. This does not have to be a death sentence. There are many ways to treat this condition.

Doctors almost universally hate chiropractors. Chiropractic patients love them. Chiropractors are experts in relieving pain through manipulation of the spine. Relief is often wonderful but temporary. Short term relief is better than no relief at all.

The ancient art of acupuncture can also be effective at reducing pain. Needles are inserted in the body in a fashion to provide relief. Before you try acupuncture make sure they use new needles on each patient. Old needles will put you at risk of HIV infection.

Another method of pain relief is through visualization. For this to work you need complete peace and quiet. Sit in your most comfortable chair. For example if your arm is in pain imagine it bright red. Close your eyes and breathe slowly and deeply. Imagine you are turning a dial in your mind. You turn the dial slowly and your arm becomes a lighter shade of red. You can feel the pain leave your body. As you continue to turn the dial your arm is now pink and is in less pain. Gradually over fifteen minutes you turn the dial all the way and your arm becomes white and pain free. The more you practice this technique the more effective it will be.

Many doctors don't seem sympathetic to pain patients. They seem to believe in the Puritan philosophy that suffering is good. It's easy for them to feel this way because they're not in agony. You should insist on having a doctor that treats your pain aggressively. A pain clinic can often be the answer. Doctors there are experienced in relieving suffering. They will provide you with the medication you need.

Narcotics are the best pain relievers. Many doctors won't prescribe them because they are afraid their patients may become addicted. Pain clinic doctors understand the risks and rewards of narcotics. It is believed that a patient in severe chronic pain can take narcotics for many years without serious addiction problems. Narcotics can give you back your life and allow you to function. It is a decision only you and your pain specialist can make.

As you can tell from the above, chronic pain is not a hopeless situation. Treatment at a pain clinic can greatly improve your ability to function. Joining a pain support group is always helpful. With proper treatment, your life can be as rich and productive as before your injury.

Infidelity

Don't cheat on your spouse. Trust is the cornerstone of any relationship. A marriage is built on fidelity. When one partner is unfaithful confidence in the entire union is destroyed.

What should you do if your spouse is unfaithful to you? Should you try to save the marriage? The decision is entirely up to you. However, you should be warned that once infidelity has been committed the marriage can never be the same. You will never completely trust your partner again. You may choose to stay together out of friendship or mutual concern for the children but true romantic love will be a thing of the past. As long as both partners are faithful the couple believes they will be there for each other come what may. Infidelity destroys the confidence in this outlook.

If your partner is unfaithful a second time you should seriously consider terminating the relationship. Repeated acts represent a pattern of behavior. Why would you want to expose yourself to this kind of abuse? You may say to yourself, "I need to stay married for financial reasons." What's the current price of self-respect?

When you are married your libido doesn't disappear. You may be tempted to be unfaithful. The solution lies in a combination of foresight, common sense and self-control. Don't put yourself in compromising positions. Don't give yourself the chance to make a terrible mistake. Focus on your family and remember what they mean to you. You can destroy your entire world with one bad decision.

Domestic Abuse

There is nothing wrong with leaving your partner after one attack. If you decide to stay, tell the abuser that you will leave them forever if it ever happens again. Suggest counseling and anger management. If you are abused again follow through on your promise and terminate the relationship. Have a plan of who you would stay with and how you could get some cash before another incident happens. Unfortunately, abuse is rarely a one-shot deal without treatment.

What if verbal and emotional abuse drives you to the brink of physical abuse? The answer is to leave an argument before your temper gets the best of you. Simply tell your partner if you are getting enraged that you will finish the discussion later. By the time you return cooler heads will prevail. What's the best way to fight with your wife? Grab your hat and get as far away as possible. If this occurs regularly you should consider the viability of the relationship. Why would you want to be involved with someone to angers you to the point of violence? Try counseling. It may save your relationship and your life.

Job Loss/Unemployment

Nobody is guaranteed lifetime employment. Everyone's job is at risk. Many people will be fired because of layoffs, performance or attendance sometime in their life. Prepare for this possible eventuality by saving at least six month's pay in an emergency fund. This money should be in an interest-bearing account such as a money market fund—not in the stock market. The emergency fund prevents panic after job loss. Without it you may be forced to take the first job offered which could seriously hinder your future.

A job loss can be damaging emotionally. It is a blow to the ego. You may feel ashamed and personally rejected. It is a mistake to take such a situation personally. You were let go because of a cut-back or unsatisfactory professional performance. Your company did not reject you as a human being. You simply were no longer seen as a good fit for your position. Try to learn from the experience and take the knowledge to your next endeavor.

Of course there are some financial issues to consider after a job loss. You should negotiate the best severance package possible from your company. You should apply for unemployment insurance immediately. It takes several weeks for your application to be processed. There is no shame in collecting this benefit. You have earned this right by contributing to the unemployment insurance fund through payroll tax. Since you don't know how long it will be until your next job, it is wise to adopt a strict family budget. Concentrate on just the necessities until your situation improves. If you are ineligible for unemployment you may want to work part time to generate some income. Make sure these efforts don't interfere with your job search. For example, driving a cab or waitressing in off-hours can help you stay active and maintain your self-esteem.

Don't be devastated when you lose your job. It may end up being the best thing that ever happened to you. You may start your own business or find a much better job. Many wealthy people founded their companies when they were fired. If you didn't like your last job consider other fields. Use this challenge to motivate you and to find a better opportunity.

Drug Abuse

Drug abuse is one of the most serious domestic problems in the United States. The government has attempted to fight the war on drugs through aggressive enforcement. This plan of attack has failed miserably. The enforcement caused the price of street drugs to rise and the emergence of the highly addictive crack cocaine. Budget constraints forced many local governments to have to decide between drug rehab centers and added police. Unfortunately most opted for added enforcement instead of treatment. This decision has caused the jails in our cities to overflow with drug-related criminals. Many of these people belong in rehabilitation centers, not in prison.

Drug addiction refers to a lifestyle characterized by compulsive use of a drug. Addiction also implies the risk of harm and the need to stop drug use before the inevitable destruction of the addict's life. Drug dependence can be psychological or physical. Psychological dependence refers to the feelings of pleasure one gets from the drug use or the avoidance of discomfort. Physical dependence is the adaptation to a drug, accompanied by the development of tolerance and manifested by withdrawal. Withdrawal is characterized by physiological changes when the drug is discontinued. Popular drugs such as cocaine, marijuana and amphetamines cause psychological dependence. No physical withdrawal syndrome is experienced when these drugs are discontinued. However, withdrawal is still very difficult. Drugs such as narcotics and barbiturates cause physical and psychological dependence. Physical withdrawal symptoms follow discontinued use.

Nobody wants to be addicted to drugs. Many people feel no compassion for addicts. This position is short-sighted because no family is immune to drug problems. Not all drug addictions stem from recreational use. Anyone can have surgery and then find that they've grown dependent on the postoperative pain killers.

What should you do if you become addicted to drugs? There are too many different kinds of drugs to detail each withdrawal method. You should always seek the help of a doctor before discontinuing the drug use. This is because withdrawal from some drugs is dangerous and must be done in a hospital setting. Also, the doctor may give you medications to ease your discomfort. These medications make withdrawal from even heroin very viable.

Abstinence is a bigger challenge than withdrawal for most people. Narcotics Anonymous (N.A.) suggests that the addict changes people, places and things. You must avoid your friends that are still using drugs. Don't return to your old environment and habits. If you wish to remain sober you have to start a new life. Attending N.A. meetings is very helpful. You benefit from the support and advice of others. N.A. has meetings in virtually every town in the country. Simply call information to determine the closest location.

Alcohol Abuse

Seven out of ten Americans drink alcohol. One out of ten will have problems with alcoholism. Alcoholism is characterized by a destructive pattern of behavior associated with drinking. The individual's ability to work is impaired. Marriage failure and job loss can occur. Alcoholics might be arrested for DWI or public drunkenness. The individual may be hospitalized for liver problems.

Alcohol differs from other drugs only by its legality and cultural acceptance. Taken in excess it is extremely damaging to bodily systems. Alcohol is toxic to all the internal organs including the brain and heart muscle. If you think you drink too much you should take the appropriate steps to quit. Denial is of the biggest road blocks to quitting drinking. Thus, seek help if a friend or family member suggests it, even if you don't think you are abusing alcohol.

You should first alert your doctor that you're planning to stop drinking. He or she will be thrilled at the news. He/she will probably prescribe some medication to make your withdrawal easier. When heavy alcohol use is discontinued it is followed by severe withdrawal. The medication your doctor will prescribe can virtually eliminate all discomfort during this difficult time.

As with other drugs, abstinence is more difficult than withdrawal. Alcoholics Anonymous (A.A.) can be a big part of the solution. A.A. provides the alcoholic with sober associates who are always available as well as an area in which to socialize away from the bar. If you really want to stay sober, you'll have to associate with non-drinking friends.

Therapy can also be a big help. Even if you've stopped drinking, you will still have to deal with the problems in your life that were associated with drinking. A counselor can help you figure out solutions to some of these issues.

Smoking

There is virtually nothing more unhealthy than smoking cigarettes. Cigarettes kill more people than all other drugs put together. If the government didn't profit so much, cigarettes would certainly be illegal. Cigarettes are one of the leading causes of cancer, heart disease and stroke. If you smoke, you have a life expectancy of at least ten years less than a nonsmoker.

It is not too late to quit smoking. If you discontinue smoking for more than two years your risk of heart attack is reduced to the level of those who never smoked. You will also enjoy improved lung capacity.

It is very difficult to quit smoking. However, people do it every day. You can join their ranks through concentrated effort. Try nicotine gum, the patch, hypnosis and counseling. Try every available therapy until you achieve success. Spare no expense. The rewards of quitting are too important.

Illness

Everyone can expect to experience periods of bad health in their lives. You need a good doctor. Your doctor should be knowledgeable and caring. He/she should be willing to spend time with you and thoroughly explain your condition. Don't hire a doctor who doesn't listen patiently to your concerns. Don't hire a doctor that won't write proper medication for your symptoms. You must have total confidence in your physician.

If you trust your doctor, you won't panic when illness strikes. A calm head is the secret to dealing with this form of adversity. Your doctor should be able to give you an accurate diagnosis and explain the process of your recovery fully. This information should ease your mind. You may not be able to be completely functional until you are recovered but you won't be weighed down with worry.

Make the best of your weakened condition. Rent some movies that you've been interested in seeing. Read a book that you've been meaning to read. Before you know it you'll be back at work in the hectic world so try to enjoy your respite as much as possible.

Financial Loss

Most people experience financial collapse at least once in their life. Yours could be caused by a stock market crash, business failure, lawsuit or other fiscal disaster. The nest egg that you've worked years to accumulate is suddenly destroyed overnight. You are mired in depression. What should you do?

The first thing you should do is to attempt to put the loss in perspective. You may feel you have nothing in the world. Is that true? Take inventory of your life. Sit down and write all of your assets on a piece of paper. You may have a family that loves you. You may have good health. You may have friends. You may be glad to live in a well-developed country like the United States. It won't take long for you to realize that your most valuable assets aren't monetary.

Next determine why you had a financial collapse. Was it bad luck? Were you reckless? It is important in life to expect the best but also prepare for the worst. Diversify your assets to attempt to prevent these devastating losses. Bad luck doesn't make you a bad person. Don't give up. The skills you've acquired over the years will enable you to rebuild your wealth.

Ailing Parent

If you are lucky, you will have elderly parents some day. At some point, they may need your care and support. You should want to help them out of love and loyalty. You should help them because you want to, not because you are obligated. *If you help them because of love instead of guilt you will handle the situation better emotionally.*

Help your parents, but don't let them monopolize your life. Sometimes older parents forget that you have your own life to lead and expect you to spend all your time with them. Don't let them make you feel guilty. Take care of them, but make sure you enjoy your own life.

The secret with dealing with an ailing parent is patience. They tend to be set in their ways. You will too when you reach that age. Don't argue with them. They will rarely admit they're mistaken. Be patient and encourage whatever is in their best interest. Ailing parents (like other suffering people) can be snappish. Don't take it personally if they insult you. Their behavior may be a result of their physical pain. If they are offensive simply excuse yourself from the room.

Sometimes older people tend to babble excessively. Try to be a good son/daughter and patiently listen to them. Remember you are making their day by listening to them. One helpful tip when listening to the same story over and over again is to remember that storytelling and the memories associated with them are part of your parents' identity. It is what gives meaning to their lives. An extra ten minutes of listening won't kill you. You'll end up telling your kids the same stories so they know about their grandparents. This will give them a sense of family lineage.

Do your best to help your ailing parents. Old age can be a miserable experience. Try to be patient and sympathetic toward them. Someday you might be in their shoes. If you provide love and support for an ailing parent, you will feel good about yourself long after they are gone.

Mental Illness

There is no shame in mental illness. Many psychological disorders are chemical or hormonal and can be treated easily with medication. Other difficulties are simply a normal reaction (anger, sadness, anxiety) to extreme events (trauma, stress, loss, etc.). Don't let your embarrassment stand in the way of your mental health.

Everyone feels sad or depressed at times. Clinical depression can be defined as an emotional state characterized by exaggerated feelings of sadness, melancholy, dejection, helplessness and hopelessness. It differs from the common "down in the dumps" mood in the duration (how long) and the severity (how bad). If you find yourself in this condition frequently, see your doctor without delay. He or she may suggest counseling. There are also very effective medications to treat certain types of this disorder. Research indicates that therapy with medication works better than either treatment or medication by itself, especially for a chemical depression.

Everyone experiences significant anxiety at some point in his or her life. Mild anxiety heightens the use of capacity. Panic states severely hinder overall functioning. Anxiety manifests itself as a state of uneasiness, apprehension, uncertainty and fear. This is usually the result of the anticipation of some threat or danger, usually of an intrapsychic nature, rather than of external origin. In extreme cases, the overwhelming emotional discomfort is accompanied by physical reactions such as rapid pulse, shortness of breath, high blood pressure, hyperventilation and profuse sweating. There are medications that can control the symptoms of anxiety. Counseling is also beneficial. Counseling will help you with coping skills that will reassure you that you can deal with your problems and any ensuing panic reaction. Sometimes, just knowing why you had a panic attack prevents future ones. Furthermore, many people have more anxiety about having another attack than the problem that originally caused the panic attack.

Death

Death is the one thing you have in common with everyone else in the world. No one likes to discuss this topic. We even use euphemisms such as life insurance. Isn't it really death insurance? You can prepare for the death of both yourself and your loved ones. This preparation will prevent much suffering in the future. Try to cultivate a belief in the afterlife so you will not be as crushed when a loved one passes away. People who know where they're going aren't afraid to leave.

No matter how well prepared you are, you will experience grief when a loved one dies. To recover from your loss, you must express your feelings. Crying removes toxins that are produced by emotional shock. Remember, feeling and expressing loss is emotionally healing. Those people who repress or deny feelings of loss end up numbing themselves. You may not outwardly feel pain, but it is still there. In addition, this numb state will diminish feelings of joy. The natural grieving process can take a long time. *It is difficult to shorten the grieving process but you can reduce its pain.*

1. You should not be embarrassed to receive counseling for your sadness.

2. Joining a support group and being with others who have faced a similar loss can be helpful.

3. Remember the person who passed away is no longer suffering any physical pain.

4. The loved one who died would not want you to live the rest of your life in agony.

5. Remember the time you spent with the deceased fondly.

6. They remain alive in your heart. You were lucky to know them.

7. Take a part of them with you. If your parent or friend was known for a certain quality, try to act as they did in this area.

8. Appreciate people while they are still alive. Work on your relationships before it is too late.

9. Spend time comforting the dying person. Express your love. Say good-bye.

Terminal Illness

What if you are diagnosed with a terminal illness? You are perfectly justified in thinking that life isn't fair. Prayer, support groups, counseling and medication can ease your emotional pain. Try to be thankful for the time you have had and make the most of your remaining days. It is comforting for many in this position to get their financial affairs in order. With proper medical care your physical suffering should be limited. Be sure you have a compassionate doctor who will prescribe you proper pain relieving medication. You've been dealt a bad card, but through prayer reassure yourself that you are moving on to a better place.

A much bigger tragedy than your own demise would be the death of your child. When people die out of sequence it is unnatural. Burying a child is the hardest thing anyone can do. This pain will stay with you in some form for the rest of your life.

There are methods to relieve the intensity of your agony. Join a support group and receive counseling. Remain as active as possible. Your agony will ease over time to some degree. Understandably, a part of you will always be upset and bitter about your loss. Pray to God for strength. Remember your child would not want you to remain in mourning forever. He/she would want you to have an enjoyable life. Your happiness doesn't mean you don't care for or miss your child.

Hopefully, the suggestions from this chapter can save you heartache, time and trouble. After all, that's why you're reading this book in the first place—isn't it?

FAITH

It may be politically incorrect to discuss religion and faith. However *The Secrets of Life* would be incomplete without a discussion of the power of faith. Don't worry if you are a non-believer or uncertain about faith. This will not be a recruiting session. This chapter will simply point out the benefits of cultivating a connection with God. The power of faith on the human mind is well documented. Consider the confidence levels of two individuals going through hard times. The first feels he/she is standing alone in a hurricane. The second feels he/she is anchored and backed by the power of Almighty God. Who do you think is more likely to achieve a favorable result?

Whatever you do, don't think you're too smart to believe in God. Five hundred years ago all of the "smart" people thought the world was flat. A hundred years ago "smart" people laughed at the idea of bacteria causing infections. Consider the order and complexity of the world and it's not difficult to comprehend a Creator. Try to cultivate the ability to believe in abstract concepts. This skill will help you in all areas of life. It will make you a more creative individual. Those who believe in only what they can see often miss out on the whole picture.

Faith can provide comfort during life's darkest moments. If

everyone else abandons you, you are still not alone if you trust in God.

You don't have to believe in God if you don't want to, but imagine the possibilities if you did. Wouldn't it be nicer to believe you're going to heaven rather than just being a pile of bones in a coffin when you die? What's the downside? Faith costs you nothing and reaps great spiritual rewards.

What if you believe in God but don't feel close to Him? This situation is easily remedied. Prayer is the answer. Currently you probably only pray to God when you are in a jam. Prayer, like any other skill, needs to be practiced. The more you speak with your Creator the more confident you will become that He is listening. Ask for guidance, strength, peace and protection. By thanking God each day in your prayers you will feel more blessed and happy.

Faith has other fantastic benefits. Faith leads many people to public worship. These services can be a great source of friendship and support. As a general rule, you'll meet better people at church than at the bars. Many happy marriages began as friendships at church or synagogue. Attending worship services can give you a feeling of connection with humankind. You may be so busy that you think you don't have an hour a week to spare. It may benefit you to reconsider this position. Membership in a church or synagogue can provide you with great joy and be an important part of your life. By now, the benefits of faith in God should be obvious to you. Trust in God but don't forget to have faith in yourself. Realize that with God's help you can handle all of life's challenges. When you reach this conclusion, you will find a peace greater than you have ever known.

CONCLUSION

You have completed this book and now know *The Secrets of Life*. You now possess an arsenal of practical methods to help you in all facets of day-to-day living. Knowledge of these solutions is not enough. Please practice the valuable techniques outlined in this volume until you master life's mysteries. We wrote this book to save people time and trouble. We wanted you to obtain a lifetime of knowledge without a lifetime of painful mistakes. We have absolute trust in the techniques described in *The Secrets of Life*. They are the product of two decades of research and experience. They have been tested in the laboratory of life and have been proven reliable.

Think of this work as your lifetime coach and friend. Review the appropriate chapters when the situation warrants. Master the practical techniques in this book and you will become a happier, healthier and more successful person than you ever thought possible. Your greatest dreams of the past will seem minor compared to your powerful new realities. Go out and conquer the world. Wisdom is your weapon. You are armed with *The Secrets of Life*.

John Alkalay, Psy.D.
William Trautwein